Rita (Tkatschow) Hill

Born under
the Hammer and Sickle

From Communist Russia to Freedom in Canada

ISBN: 978-1-4866-2618-2
eBook ISBN: 978-1-4866-2619-9

Word Alive Press
119 De Baets Street Winnipeg, MB R2J 3R9
www.wordalivepress.ca

WORD ALIVE
—P R E S S—

Cataloguing in Publication information can be obtained from Library and Archives Canada.

In *Born under the Hammer and Sickle,* Rita Hill tells the engaging story of her family's war-time journey from Russia, to Germany, and finally to Canada. This is a memorable story of God's gracious protection and provision for Rita's life. Highly recommended.

—Dr. Rick Reed
Chancellor, Heritage College and Seminary

Rita Hill's life journey mirrors my own mother's experiences as a young child growing up in Josef Stalin's Soviet Union. In many ways, their stories are intertwined, both by kinship and by their Christian faith. Like Rita's family, mine was grateful to be able to successfully flee the ravages of Stalin's regime, only to experience the horrors and displacement of wartime Germany. In both cases, Rita and my mother and their families found sanctuary here in Canada— Winnipeg to be exact—and made new lives for themselves in their adopted home. This book serves as a reminder of the tenuousness of life and the fragility of our freedoms. Thank you, Rita, for reminding us of the abiding love of our Creator and the freedom we can all experience through His grace and provision in our lives.

Bravo on a story of inspiration and hope!
—Hon. Ed Fast, MP (Abbotsford)

To my grandchildren:
Jordan and his wife, Catherine,
Patrick, and Nathalie.

Contents

Acknowledgements   ix

One: Early Childhood   1

Two: Occupation by the German Forces
and Evacuation to Germany   29

Three: Germany: Life in the Refugee Camp   41

Four: The End of the War   59

Five: Life in Backnang   91

Six: Oh Canada, Here We Come!   101

Seven: Ottawa   117

Epilogue   125

Acknowledgements

I would like to thank all the people who have encouraged me to have my story published. I started to write my memoirs ten years ago, and then, due to different circumstances and our downsizing to a new home, this was set aside for a "more opportune time."

It was during recent months that my family and friends got after me again to work on my memoirs and have them published. One couple in particular, our dear holiday travel companions, Dave and Carolynn Robertson, would so often ask during our phone conversations how my book was coming along. I can finally say that I have finished writing it.

Special thanks go to my husband, Sam, who kept constantly encouraging me during the times of my frustrations. Thanks to Scott McClare who used his editing skills to spot errors or to suggest any changes or additions to my script before handing it in to the publishers.

I couldn't have done without the help of my son-in-law Chris Purdy, who kept my laptop in working order.

Thanks to Matthew Weston, also my son-in-law, who did a beautiful job with my photo.

I love giving and receiving hugs, so to all of my encouragers and helpers: consider yourself hugged.

One

Early Childhood

It was after midnight. There was a knock on the door. Papa made his way to the door and asked, "Who is it? What do you want?"

"NKVD. Open the door," was the answer.

When Papa turned on the outside light and opened the door, he saw two men standing there, demanding, "Get the ladder for that house. We want to see what you are hiding up in the attic."

They were pointing to the little house a few yards from the new brick house we were living in. That little house, consisting of two rooms, was purchased by my parents to live in after they got married.

Papa slipped his feet into the shoes he had left near the door earlier and walked over to the little house where he kept the ladder, all along being followed by the two men, who held flashlights in their hands. He picked up the ladder, walked with it to the end of the house, and leaned it against the wall, with the top up against a small door that opened to the inside.

One of the men climbed the ladder and, after pushing the door in, stuck his arm with the flashlight into the attic and made a couple of circles, so the light reached every corner of the attic. Then he came back down the ladder and motioned to his partner with his hand, saying, "Nothing." After this, both of them left without saying anything to Papa.

The NKVD was the Soviet government's secret police organization from 1934 to 1946, the predecessor of the KGB. In a way, Papa was not really surprised to have them come to check on him. This happened quite often to people in Kichkas, our hometown. However, it was still a terrifying experience for my parents. Papa could have been arrested and taken away from us that night, had they found what they were looking for. He often wondered what the real reason for their sudden appearance was. Did he have an enemy in Kichkas who harboured a dislike for him and conjured a lie to the authorities to get him into trouble? After all, at the regular Communist meetings in town, the attendees were encouraged to watch each other and report the names of people they suspected of disloyalty to the regime. Stalin, being an atheist, was particularly suspicious of people of faith and of the ethnic groups of that day. There was a great population of German-speaking citizens in our town, as well as in the surrounding towns that were planted on the west shore of the Dniepr River. These were the enemies and potential troublemakers that could cause political dissent and another revolution. They had to be done away with. It followed, therefore, that there were a lot of arrests—usually in the middle of the night. In the mornings, weeping women would disclose to friends and relatives that their loved ones had been taken away during the night, and almost never heard from again. The term used in town was: "he disappeared." These people were thrown into prisons, tortured, or sent to Siberia to do hard labour.

Of my mother's six brothers, four were taken from their families. Peter was imprisoned. Jakob was shot; he most likely objected to his arrest. Heinrich was sent to Siberia. And the fourth, my Uncle Kornelius, just "disappeared." No one knew what happened to him. He was arrested a few days prior to the German occupation of our town.

How the families without a father were supposed to survive was not the state's concern. The now-single moms had to find a way to provide for their children, by taking on jobs or selling everything they had in order to buy food.

My father was blacklisted as well, and had it not been for the sudden invasion into our town by the German army in 1941, he, too, would have been arrested. One possible reason was that Papa refused to join the Communist Party. Many of the men in our town were party members. They held regular meetings, which every adult had to attend, whether or not they were party members. At these meetings, they were indoctrinated with Communist propaganda.

Another reason Papa was not trusted was that he was married to a "foreigner." My mother was of German Dutch heritage, but she was born in Russia and was a Russian citizen. Her ancestors had settled in Russia over a hundred years before she was born.

Afterward, my family immigrated to Canada, and my parents settled in B.C. In the 1970s, Mama received a letter from an acquaintance in Russia. It said her brother Heinrich had been released from the labour camps in Siberia, sick in body and broken in spirit. Though he was in his eighties, he had somehow made his way back to Kichkas. When he got there, his family was gone; they had been evacuated to Germany by the German forces during the war. His house was occupied by strangers. There was no one left in town whom he knew—and no one who still remembered him—other than an elderly couple who remembered him from many years before. They took him in and gave him a place to stay, knowing that his life was coming to an end.

The only thing Heinrich brought with him was a rough-looking copy of a manuscript that he had worked on for years, describing life in the hard labour camps of Siberia. His intention was to have it published someday and to have the proceeds of the book go to his surviving family. Heinrich knew that his life on earth was short. He asked his benefactors to store it safely away and, in due time, after his death, to have it published. After Heinrich died, the couple who had offered him a place to stay while he was sick now had second thoughts about harbouring a document that might cause them trouble, if discovered. They decided the best way to get rid of it was to burn it, so as not to leave any traces—and that's what they did, page by page.

This is only one story of many that are still out there somewhere, stories of the inmates of the hard labour camps who were innocent sufferers because of Stalin's paranoid personality. It was during this time of unrest in the Soviet Union that Papa's parents moved from Moscow to the Zaporizhzhia area. Not much is known about his ancestry. Papa's father's name was Michael Tkatschow, and he worked on the railroads in Kichkas, our hometown. It was a suburb of Zaporizhzhia, situated on the west shores of the Dniepr River.

Papa's mother's name was Varvara. She and her husband raised their four sons on a small farm. My father, Sergey, was the second youngest of four sons, and he graduated from the institute of agronomy.

Mama's name was Maria Martens. Papa called her "Marusia," an endearing Russian name for Maria. Speaking Russian was no problem for her, as she was educated in both the German and Russian languages. Her ancestors were Mennonites who had left Switzerland and southern Germany in 1530 because of religious persecution and had made their homes in Belgium and Holland for several years. From there they settled in Prussia (now Poland). When the Tsarina, Catherine the Great of Russia, heard about the Mennonites' farming skills and good work habits, she invited them to settle in her country. She promised them lots of land, and instead of having the men take up arms during the war, allowed them to join the armed forces as medics and peacekeepers.

Mama's ancestors first arrived with their wagons on Khortitza, an island close to Kichkas, which was part of southern Russia in 1789 and is now part of Ukraine. After finding a place for their wagons, they drank coffee in the shade of an oak tree. Pictures of that tree can be seen today in history books of the Mennonite settlers in Russia. It was 150 years old when I saw it. Its trunk was so big that it took ten children holding hands to encircle it. It had a metal fence around it, and a plaque was attached with an inscription that told the story of the Mennonite settlers. They settled in an area a few kilometres from Khortitza near the Dniepr River, and they called it Einlage, after the place in Prussia from where they had last emigrated.

The Dniepr River was very much an attraction for the families that settled nearby. Picnics were held on its banks, which were covered with all kinds of flowers in the summer, and children showed off their diving skills by jumping into the river from the high cliffs along its shores. Mama spoke of the times when she and her sisters would climb up on a rock called "Monkey's Head," so called because of its shape, and jump down into the water. Occasionally there would be a drowning when somebody ventured into an area where the undercurrents were strong enough to pull one under.

In 1924–25, seven years after the 1917–18 revolution, the original town of Einlage was flooded in preparation for the construction of a hydroelectric power dam that would span the Dniepr River. The people of Einlage were moved upward to higher ground, where they settled in an area they called the New Einlage, the Russian name for which was Kichkas. That is where I was born.

Kichkas was surrounded by several small towns, and the whole area was called Robochiy Posiolok (Workers

Settlement). The area was given that name because of the influx of manpower needed to work on the hydroelectric power dam. Work began in 1927, and it was finished in October of 1932, just half a year before I was born. In 1941, during World War II when the Soviets were retreating during the advance of the German forces, they blew up the dam in the middle. It was repaired during the German occupation, but then it was blown up again when the Germans retreated. It was eventually reconstructed to its original state after the end of the war.

The first house we lived in seemed to get smaller as our family kept growing. My brother Valentin (Val) was two and a half years old by the time I was born. So now we were a family of four living in a house that measured eight by six metres, and it consisted of a kitchen and a living room/bedroom. It had a total of two windows, one in each room. The attic was accessible by ladder from the outside, where there was a small door in the peak of the roof. It was used to store a few things for which there was no room in the house. In our town, you could not store anything outside because theft at night was a common occurrence. The houses in our area had no indoor plumbing. We had an outhouse between our house and the fruit garden, and there was a drawing well in the yard that supplied us with our daily water needs.

I was not yet born when Papa started making plans to build a larger house on the property that would accommodate our growing family. The earth for the basement was excavated, and building material arrived slowly. My younger brother, Alexander, was born four years after my arrival. We called him Sasha, and later he was called Alex. The living space in the house was now bulging, with two adults and three children living in it. I was six years old when we moved into our new brick house. It took Papa seven years to finish building it because funds were short and building materials were slow to come after orders were placed.

The new house was situated a few yards from the small house, with the front of the house facing the garden instead of the street. This is the way the houses in our town were built, to discourage break-ins. There were four steps that led to the landing in front of the door. On both sides of the steps and the landing was a wrought iron railing. Mama kept a potted oleander tree on the landing, and it was stolen one night in spite of our property being all fenced in along the street.

Our new house consisted of a living room, an eat-in kitchen, two bedrooms, and a large pantry. There were seven windows in total. In the pantry were steps leading to the attic and cellar. The attic had two dormer windows and enough space for future bedrooms for the children. On many occasions, I would go up to the attic and look out the dormer windows to watch what was going on in the neighbourhood yards. With the sun shining in, it was nice and warm up there.

To get into the cellar, you had to lift a trap door in the middle of the pantry floor, walk down several steps, and then feel your way in the dark for the string that hung from the ceiling. By pulling the string, a single light bulb gave enough light for us to see the shelves that lined the walls of the damp cellar. Papa stored the apples there that ripened in the winter. Each apple was wrapped in paper and arranged on the shelves in single layers. In the winter they would be used for bedtime snacks. They tasted just like the Granny Smith apples we buy in the grocery stores here in Canada. I can still see my maternal grandmother, whom we called Grandmama, scraping an apple for herself with a small knife in order to be able to eat it. She had no teeth, and she refused to wear her dentures because they felt uncomfortable.

After moving into the new house, the small house was used as a summer kitchen, and in winter it was used to store coal for our furnace. As mentioned previously, our water came from the drawing well situated at one end of our back yard. This water served us for drinking, cooking, doing laundry, and bathing. We had no refrigeration in the house, so to keep the dairy products fresh in the summer, Mama would store the milk, cream, butter, and cheese in a covered hole that was dug about a foot into the ground. It had a cover over it and was topped with a rock to keep any animals away. We called it our summer cooler.

The outhouse stood hidden behind some trees. In it was a seat for grownups as well as a smaller one for the children. If any of us children had to go to the washroom in the middle of the night, we would have to use a covered chamber pot that sat under one of the beds. I was always nervous having to use the outhouse because of a neighbour who was insane. He would stand behind our fence near the outhouse at any time of the day, and just stare into our garden. Sometimes he came to the door and knocked until Mama opened the door to see who was there. Then he would stand right in the doorway and try to engage Mama in a conversation about space matters. He told her all about flying saucers. Mama kept quiet, but she felt quite uncomfortable during those times. However, there was nothing that she could do but wait until he ran out of words and left. Twice, when he was placed in a facility for insane people, he escaped and returned to his house next door. Eventually he disappeared, so I presume that a more secure place was found for him.

The chore of doing laundry in our house usually lasted two days. Mama hired a peasant woman from the village to come in the evening to start the process. I watched her grate the homemade soap into a large round metal tub that was filled with hot water. Then the laundry was added, and it would soak all night. The following day, the peasant woman returned and scrubbed the laundry on a washboard. The dark items were rinsed and hung out to dry. The whites were put into a large cast-iron vat that was built into the hearth. Cold water was added to it, and when it came to a boiling point, some more of the grated soap was added. After sufficient boiling, the laundry was rinsed once, and then to a second rinse, Mama added a few drops of bluing, which made everything look bright white. Then everything was hung on the clothesline that stretched for many yards from post to post, supported by poles every few feet. After the items were dry, they were brought into the house, and Mama would iron the sheets, pillow slips, and tablecloths by using a hand mangle. That is a process that is no longer used today.

We had a fruit orchard consisting of 162 trees. The garden was bordered with fifty-two cherry trees on each side. These cherries were sour and good for making pies and preserves. The rest of the garden consisted of eighteen Bing cherry trees (several of the white variety), sixteen apple trees, fourteen pear trees, forty-three apricot trees, and nineteen plum trees (consisting of four varieties).[1] Having studied agronomy and horticulture, Papa was always trying to find a new type of fruit tree to add to his garden. These were usually imported from other countries. One year he imported two new trees, the fruit of which was smaller than a peach but larger than an apricot. One of these trees he planted in the garden, and the other he planted against the brick wall of the house where the sun shone most of the day. He removed all the front and back branches, and only left the side branches, which he spread out on each side of the trunk and fastened flat against the wall. This kind of planting is called "espalier." In our town, I don't know of anyone who had one like it. When these trees finally bore some fruit, it was "hands off" for the family until Papa closely inspected its shape and colour, and he was the first one to have a taste of it.

---

[1] During my childhood, I had no knowledge of the quantities of trees and bushes in our garden. It was only while going through Papa's papers, after his death, that I found this information. Papa was very good at keeping a journal of things and events, and his memory was perfect until he passed away.

Papa also planted a large vineyard with thirty-two vines and three different types of grapes. Between the two houses, we had a raspberry patch. In the front part of the garden, there were nineteen gooseberry bushes, and under some of the fruit trees bordering the well, we had red and black currant bushes. At Easter time, my parents would hide coloured eggs in these bushes for us to find.

The year before we were evacuated to Germany, Papa's last experiment was with peanuts. He planted several hills of them, and he had an abundant harvest beyond his expectation.

To walk through the garden during blossom time was an awesome experience. The scent was overwhelming. Many a time, I would lie under a tree and daydream. I would look up at the sky and wonder what was beyond those clouds. If God lived there, what did he look like? I never asked my parents any of those questions. My parents did not talk to us about God. It wasn't that they didn't have any faith themselves: Papa was of Russian Orthodox background, and Mama had become a Christian when she was a teenager after a travelling evangelist visited their village, and she heard him speak about Jesus, whom God sent to this earth to be our Saviour. After the revolution, when Communism took over and the country became atheistic, most of the churches were shut down, and it was dangerous for parents to talk to their children about God for fear of having the children removed from their home. Hence, we never heard about God.

Fruit-picking time was a busy time, as there were not enough of us in the family to get the job done. We had people come from outside our town to "pick your own" cherries. Instead of taking payment from them, they had to pick a pail of cherries for our family before they could pick one for themselves. That worked well for both them and us. We would sell some of the cherries at the market, and the rest were dried and put in sacks for the winter. Apples, pears, apricots, and plums were cut up and dried on long boards arranged like tables in our yard. These were sacked and stored for winter consumption as well. We saved the apricot pits and enjoyed them in the winter by cracking them open with a hammer on a small anvil. They tasted just like almonds.

Papa worked hard in the garden. That was usually done after he came home from work. I can still see him walking between the fruit trees with a tank strapped to his back and spraying the trees with pesticide. One year all the gardens in our area were infested with caterpillars. They approached the trees like an army on a moving conveyor belt about twenty-four inches wide. They would strip one tree naked within a short time before they moved on to the next tree. It was impossible to stop them. Each one of our family members picked the caterpillars off by handfuls and threw them into a pail. Then the pail was emptied into a hole that Papa dug. After adding some kerosene, he lit a match and threw it into the hole, and the fire killed the caterpillars.

You always knew spring had arrived when the hills and valleys on the outskirts of our town were covered with a blanket of purple crocuses. Val and I would pick a bouquet of them for Mama. After the crocuses finished blooming, there were other flowers like scillas, lilies of the valley, grape hyacinths, and violets. These grew wild in big patches. There was no shortage of tulips of every colour in our garden. Papa made sure of that. We also had several peony bushes along the path to our front gate. We didn't have any lilac bushes. I love the smell of lilacs. Some of the neighbours on our street had Persian lilacs growing along their fences, and when I walked by there, I would reach up and break off a bough and bury my nose in it.

Summertime was always a happy time. The days were never long enough for me. My friend Martha lived across the street, and her family had a cow that was sent out to pasture every morning. Sometimes, at the end of the day, I was allowed to go to the pasture with Martha when it was time to bring the cow home. On one such occasion, while waiting to retrieve Martha's cow, I waded into the river nearby to get my feet wet. Suddenly the water seemed to open up under my feet and close over my head. I had stepped into a hole. I turned quickly to one side and got out by grabbing onto some rocks. I am not a swimmer, so I was very fortunate to get out alive. Now I had a dilemma: being all wet, how would I explain the predicament to Mama after getting home? As it was, by the time we got back with the cow, my clothes were no longer dripping wet, and I got away with not having to "let the cat out of the bag," so to speak. Today, as I think of that incident, I realize that God had protected me that day, as I could easily have drowned.

When I was about six years old, it was decided that Val and I might enjoy a week at a children's camp on the island of Khortitza, just a few miles from home. Papa was able to borrow a motorcycle with a sidecar, where both Val and I were seated, each holding a bag with our few belongings in our laps, and that's the way we arrived at the camp. It was a fun week for me, even though I did not know any of the other children. I felt that as long as my brother was anywhere near me, I was OK. I loved the games that we played, and I vividly remember being blindfolded as we played pin the tail on the donkey. There were two incidents that were unpleasant: In the company of Val and several other children, we climbed a fence to pick some apricots that were not yet ripe. I can't remember about the other children, but I got sick to my stomach that night, and I wished at that moment to be home in my own bed. The other incident was when the camp nurse discovered lice on my head. I don't know how I got them, but that problem was dealt with quickly by having my hair all sheared off. It was a thoroughly humiliating experience for me, but if Mama was shocked at seeing me come home bald, she did not show it.

My favourite pastime in the summer was to play games with the other children who lived in the neighbourhood. Some days we would play tag or hide-and-seek until it got dark. I didn't like it when I heard Mama's voice calling, "Ri-i-i-ta" from our front gate. My name on the birth certificate is Margarita, but I was never called that by my parents. (Although when I went to school in Germany, I was called Margarete.)

When I got home from playing, I had to wash my and Alex's feet in a basin, as we always played barefoot outdoors, and our feet got really dirty. Before getting ready for bed, there was a special treat: a slice of dark rye bread with some lard on it. Sometimes Mama would let us go outside to pick a few plums off a tree that grew not far from the door. These plums were very large, smooth, and red in colour. As the day cooled down, they would be covered with fresh dew, and they tasted wonderful. I can't say that I like them as much today as I did when I was a child.

On nice clear nights, Val and I were allowed to sleep outdoors on boards that Mama made into a bed for us. As we lay there, we would gaze into the night sky and try to count the myriads of stars. It was very quiet, and the only sound was the rustling of the leaves as a breeze would blow through the trees. You could hear the occasional barking of dogs in the distance. It didn't take us long to fall asleep.

Celebrating Christmas was not allowed by the Communists, so instead, everybody celebrated New Year's Day. Our parents would make sure that there was a small tree on the table, which they would decorate during the night. They used real candles that they would light in the morning, just before we children would be allowed into the living room. On the table were three plates, one for each child. Each contained a mandarin orange, cookies, some candies, and a few walnuts for us to crack open. There was also a toy for each child. We were told that Grandfather Frost had come at night and left the gifts for the children.

Occasionally Grandfather Frost appeared at our house some evening before New Year's Day to see if the children had been good. He wore a fur coat and a Siberian hat, and he had a beard just like Santa Claus. When he spoke, Val crawled under the bed because the booming voice scared him. On that occasion, I was almost three years old, but I wasn't scared because, to me, the voice of Grandfather Frost sounded familiar. While picking up the candies that Grandfather Frost had left for us, I peeked under his coat and confidently said, "It's Aunt Sarah." I must have recognized the dress that Aunt Sarah wore under the coat. Aunt Sarah wasn't really our aunt. She was just an acquaintance of our mother's, but we children always called friends of our parents "uncles" and "aunts."

In the winter, when we walked to school, we wore "valenki," felt boots, on our feet. They were made of several layers of felt stitched together. They were warm as long as they stayed dry, but by the time we made it through the snow to school, our feet were always wet. I would put my boots over the hot-water registers along the wall of my classroom, but they never dried properly, and I would arrive home with freezing wet feet. Then Mama placed them over the warm hearth where they stayed overnight, so that when morning came, they were dry, and I could wear them to school again.

After school, Val and I liked to skate on the street that had become one huge rink after a freezing rain. In our town, there was no traffic to speak of in the winter. Occasionally there would be a horse-and-buggy coming down the road, and there was always enough time to get out of its way. The only unfortunate thing that could possibly happen was one of the children deliberately bumping into another child, causing some scrapes and bruises.

Even though my parents had a busy lifestyle, they made time for pleasure as well. For some time, both of them belonged to a Ukrainian folk choir. Occasionally they took me with them to choir practice. I enjoyed listening to their singing. Most of the Ukrainian folk songs have very nice melodies, and some are very sad love songs. Today I can still remember the words to some of the songs their choir sang. During the summer months, Papa took part in the soccer matches played by the young men of our town. My parents also loved to go fishing in the Dniepr River. They would leave early in the morning, catch some fish, and be home in time to make breakfast for us before Papa had to leave for work.

Sometimes we had friends or neighbours come over for tea. At that time, my parents brought out the samovar. A samovar is a boiler with a large body on top to contain hot water, and fuel in the base to boil the water. Tea was served in tall glasses. To keep the glasses from breaking when the boiling hot tea was poured, a teaspoon was placed in each glass. Sugar cubes and slices of lemon were always on the table. Drinking tea made in a samovar was special, and during that time, many a world problem was discussed around the table.

Once in a while, we would visit some relatives that lived in a town within walking distance. My paternal grandparents lived about three kilometres away, and to get to their house, we had to walk through a railroad tunnel that was halfway between their town and ours. When I was little, I liked walking through that tunnel because I could hear my echo when I called "poohoo." Consequently, when I wanted to go and visit my Russian Grandma, I would ask Mama if we could go and see Babushka (Grandma) Poohoo. I gave her that name because of the tunnel.

During the visit with my grandparents, we were treated to roasted sunflower and pumpkin seeds while the adults were engaged in playing cards. In their house, there were a lot of electrical wires in the living room because their youngest son had a hobby of building radios. The pictures on their walls were hung so high that I would get a sore neck from staring at them. They were mainly black-and-white portraits of family members. There were also several pictures of distinguished Communist party members with many medals on their uniforms, all looking very sombre. To have these kinds of pictures on display was a custom practised in many Russian homes.

Babushka Poohoo was of the Russian Orthodox faith, so she had an icon on the wall of the Virgin Mary with the baby Jesus. At Easter, Babushka Poohoo would take a paska to church, along with some coloured Easter eggs, to have them blessed by the priest. A paska is a round loaf that we call Easter bread in Canada. Sometimes Babush-ka Poohoo would come for a short visit and would bring me some coloured hair ribbons. I always wished that my hair would grow long enough to make really long braids, but my hair never grew much past shoulder length before Mama would cut it.

Occasionally we visited Aunt Tina, one of my mother's older sisters. She had six children—five girls and one boy, who was my age. They lived in a village several miles away. Their small house was situated above a little creek that flowed through the village. There was a lot to explore. They had farm animals as well as a cat, a dog, and some rabbits. For a while, their house had dirt floors, before the wooden floors were laid. After a meal, the girls had to clean up the dishes and sweep the kitchen floor. I liked to watch them sweep the floor because they created a pretty pattern in the dirt as they swept it. Aunt Tina's five daughters were all teenagers, and I looked up to them. They were always nice to me when I visited. The youngest daughter, Lisa, taught me to embroider a bird on a little branch. I was happy to take that souvenir home and show it to Mama. I knew that she would be proud of me.

Grandmama Helene Martens came to live with us after my grandfather, Heinrich Martens, passed away. She and Grandpa had fourteen children, two of whom had died in infancy. They also raised two nephews whose parents had died of typhoid fever during the typhoid epidemic in Ukraine.

Grandmama was not a big woman. She was quite slender. She had very long, dark hair that reached her lap when she sat down to comb it. She would braid it and wrap the braids around her head and fasten them with hairpins. Sometimes she would wear her hair in a bun. On special occasions, she would wear a black velvet bow draped over the bun. That happened when she attended a wedding or went to church during the time when German churches were still allowed to be open.

When Grandmama came to live with us, she brought her own bed with her, which she shared with me. She also brought a chest of drawers, where she stored her things. A round tin box full of buttons always sat on top of the chest. One day I opened the box, and to my horror, I saw a pair of dentures in the midst of all the buttons. Now I realized why Grandmama didn't have teeth. She must have had them cut out of her mouth with her gums attached, and now she was hiding them among the buttons. I quickly put the lid on the box and hoped that no one had seen me looking in it. For a long time after, I would stare at her mouth and wonder why she would do such a thing, particularly when I could enjoy biting into an apple, but she had to grate it before she could eat it.

Grandmama also brought two paintings with her. One was of a bowl of fruit, and it hung over the chest of drawers; the other painting was of a hunter carrying two dead grouse in one hand and a rifle in the other. That painting was hung on the wall right next to where I slept. I used to fix my eyes on that painting before falling asleep.

Grandmama had no trouble climbing any of our cherry trees. She would hang a pail on a branch, and with her cane, she would pull down another branch that was loaded with cherries. In no time, she would fill the pail. Under her long dress, she always wore a quilted vest to keep warm, as there wasn't an ounce of fat on her body. Over her dress, she always wore an apron.

When she lived with us, she was in charge of us children in the absence of Mama, who was busy tending the garden or selling fruit at the market or sewing for others. We had to obey Grandmama. She was a good cook, and her special chicken noodle soup was made from scratch. We had several chickens, so she would catch one, hold it by its feet, and chop its head off on a tree stump that was used for chopping wood. Then it was soaked in boiling hot water so it could be plucked and prepared for the soup. She also made her own noodles. At lunchtime, Alex often made a fuss. He would push his chair away from the table and refuse to eat. She would slowly reach under her apron and pull out a switch that was cut from a tree. As soon as he became aware of it, he would quickly push himself back to the table and, while eating, say, "It tastes good, Grandmama." I can't remember that she ever used the switch on any of us, but there was always the possibility.

Grandmama loved her coffee. Real coffee was hard to come by in those days, and chicory was the substitute in many a household. Occasionally Grandmama received a pound of real coffee beans that came from Germany. She would grind just enough beans for a cup or two and store the rest for an occasion when one of her friends came to visit. For the real coffee, she did not use our well water but the water from a neighbourhood pump about two blocks from our house. I had to walk that distance, carrying a kettle, and pump enough water to fill it. On the way home, I always tried to walk quickly because the children living in that neighbourhood were known to be troublemakers. I was afraid some of them would grab my kettle and spill the water. The fences on both sides of that street were covered with graffiti and swear words. When I got home, I didn't say anything to Grandmama as I didn't want to upset her.

Toward the end of the summer, Papa had a load of watermelons brought to our house. They were dumped in a heap at the front of the garden. They came from an island not too far from our town, where the watermelons grew large and sweet because of its sandy soil. Mama and Grandmama scooped out the contents of the watermelons and squeezed the juice into a large vat. Then it was boiled long enough to become thick. The end result was watermelon molasses, which was used for baking.

Grandmama would often sit with me on the edge of the sidewalk, just beyond our gate, and tell stories while waiting for the town goats to return from pasture at the end of the day. She was very good at telling stories. The best ones were always about wolves. Of course, I knew the story of Little Red Riding Hood and the big bad wolf. I was afraid of wolves, although I had never ever seen any in our area, but I also knew that Grandmama was never afraid of anyone or anything—at least that is the way I thought of her. As far as wolves were concerned, she would say: "If ever a wolf comes toward you, and he opens his mouth to eat you, quickly stick your hand into his mouth as far as it will go in, grab him by the tail, and turn him inside out, just like a sock. Then the wolf's teeth will be on the outside, and he no longer can bite you." I certainly could picture my Grandmama doing that to the wolf, as I knew that she was very brave, and she would always make me laugh. So that's the way we spent the time while waiting to see the goats pass by.

We did not have any goats ourselves, but we did raise a pig every year until the fall, when it was fat enough for slaughter. I hated to hear the squeal of the pig when it was caught. Grandmama's brother, Uncle Henry, and his wife, Aunt Elisabeth, often came to help with cutting the meat into portions and making the sausages. It took a whole day to get everything done. The sausage making took the longest time. The intestines were emptied, and boiling water was poured through them several times. Then the meat was ground, and spices were added before stuffing them. After that, my father would hang them up with the hams for the smoking process. Then, with the other meat portions, he salted them away in a barrel. The fat of the pig was rendered and poured over all the meat. This was done to preserve the meat for the winter. The rest of the lard was kept for cooking and baking. Of course, for helping my parents with the butchering of the pig, Uncle Henry and Aunt Elisabeth received a portion of the meat products to take home.

I never ever saw any garbage in our house or outdoors in the yard. That was because we never had anything to throw out. There were no food leftovers. If there were any bones, the dogs got them. There were no plastic containers or cans to get rid of. There were no plastic or paper shopping bags. Any groceries we bought at the store, we carried home in our own shopping bags, which were made from fabric or strong netting. Occasionally Papa would bring home a newspaper, and after my parents were finished reading it, it would be cut up into small pieces and taken to the outhouse to be used as toilet paper. Even old clothing, if it was still in good condition, would be taken apart and made into something "new," or it would be cut into rags. Once in a while, a horse-and-buggy would come down the middle of the street, loaded with all kinds of old, rusty containers, pieces of metal sheeting, and glass. We always knew the "garbage collector" was on the way just by the noise that the loose pieces created every time the wagon hit a bump. If you wanted to get rid of any of these items, the wagon would make a stop long enough to pile them on.

In the garden, we had a huge cage that housed rabbits. In the middle of the cage was a chute that went down into a hole, where the rabbits made nests in the walls of the earth for their babies. We also had a dog and a cat. The first dog we had was a Siberian Husky whose doghouse was right under the kitchen window. In the evening, when we were having supper, the dog would jump on top of the doghouse and, with his paws placed on the window ledge, would shake his head from side to side, hoping to create enough attention and sympathy to get some of our supper. The next dog we had was of the Heinz 57 variety, and he was allowed indoors. He loved to chase rabbits. Occasionally, Papa let the rabbits out of the cage so that they could graze in the garden. When it was time to get them back into the cage, Papa called the dog, and he would round them up and chase them back into the cage. In the winter, the dog liked to stretch out on the floor in front of the hearth; our cat would place itself right across the dog's belly, and they both would sleep like that. Sometimes Val or Alex took the cat into bed with them and hid it under the blankets, much to our parents' disapproval, as they did not believe that animals should be seen on a bed.

We also had several chickens, which we were raising mainly for the eggs. We noticed on several mornings that a chicken had disappeared in the night. One night, Papa heard a commotion in the chicken coop, and when he checked, he found that a fox had dug a hole under the chain-link fence to get into the coop and steal some of the chickens. Papa soon put a stop to that by fixing the hole in the fence.

Before I was old enough to go to school, my parents taught me to read the Russian alphabet. I also learned to embroider. As I said before, it was one of my Aunt Tina's daughters who took the time to teach me how to embroider. I took great care to do the stitches all the same size. When I finished the picture, I took it home, and Mama washed and ironed it. When I started school, I took it with me, and it was displayed in a special glass case along with items made by other children. My parents were proud of me because it was unusual for a child my age to be able to embroider. Unfortunately, it was never returned to me; I was told that it had been stolen. I could not understand how this could happen when the glass case was always locked. Someone said that a teacher had taken it out of the glass case. I was very sad when it wasn't returned to me.

For first grade, I went to a Russian school in the next town, while Val went to the Ukrainian school that was just a block from our house. We always walked to school, no matter how far it was.

Papa built his own radio, and in the evenings, we would sit around the radio and listen to the news. One evening, we heard that Hitler was declaring war on Russia. In the following days, Papa got busy building a bomb shelter in our garden, as he knew that there would be air raids and the very real possibility of planes dropping bombs. There was no modern equipment available to dig the hole. As it had to be done by hand, he hired a couple of men to help him. The shelter consisted of an L-shaped space with enough room for the whole family. It was covered with wood and topped off with the earth that had been dug out of the hole. At the entrance of the shelter were several steps leading down.

When the air-raid sirens went off, my parents grabbed us children, and we all ran into the shelter. Sometimes, in order to not disturb us in our sleep, we would be taken to the shelter at bedtime where Mama had made beds on wooden shelves. It was a good thing we had a bomb shelter to go to.

When the Germans were advancing close to where we lived, there were a lot of bombings in the area. If any bombs exploded close by, you could easily be injured by shrapnel or even killed. My paternal grandparents also had a bomb shelter in their garden. On one occasion, the house next door to them was hit by a bomb. When the sirens went off before the bombing, the neighbour, who had a shelter to go to, was having a smoke in the doorway of his house. Unfortunately, he was decapitated when the bomb hit the house. Some of the shrapnel from that bomb hit the tile roof of our house and caused damage to it. None of us were hurt because we were all in our bomb shelter.

Two

Occupation by the German Forces and Evacuation to Germany

In August of 1941, my hometown became alive with German soldiers everywhere. Part of our garden was set up with tents to house several dozen of them. My parents had to give up their bedroom to the commander and move into the bedroom my two brothers shared. Our outhouse was out of bounds for the soldiers; they put up makeshift toilets among the fruit trees.

The Russian school I had attended in the neighbouring town was used as a hospital for injured German soldiers. The Ukrainian school on the corner, near our house, was used as a mess hall and a nightclub.

Soon after the German occupation, a school was opened for children of German background. So, with a little bit of tutoring before starting second grade, German became my everyday language, except when Papa came home from work. Then Russian was the household language.

I loved going to German school. My three friends, Martha, her cousin Hertha, and Rita K., lived on the same street as I did, so we would walk the long way to school together. We would often walk on the railroad tracks that wound their way through Kichkas and the next town, where our school was. It was fun to see who could stay on the tracks the longest without falling off. Of course, our parents were not aware of this.

At school, during recess, we would often play dodge-ball with my big black ball, which was the size of a bowling ball, and which I was allowed to take with me to school. One day, while playing with it at home, I had to use the outhouse. I put it next to me near the bigger toilet seat, and it rolled into the toilet. Papa fished it out and cleaned it all up for me. If it retained the outhouse smell, I can't remember. I was just glad that I had my ball back.

I had a doll that was the size of a newborn baby. It was given to me for one of my early birthdays. I already had a cradle that my grandfather Heinrich had made short-ly before he passed away. He had painted it a dark green colour, and it was big enough to hold a real baby, but I used it for the doll. Mama, being a seamstress, made the bedding for it and also made baby clothes and a blanket. When I wasn't playing with my friends, I would spend my time playing with the baby doll.

Papa was a smoker during my childhood years, as was my friend Martha's father. Cigarettes were hard to come by during the war, so Papa rolled his own, while Martha's dad smoked a pipe. Among the German army, there were a lot of smokers, so there were a lot of cigarette butts lying around everywhere. Martha and I picked up the discard-ed butts, shook the leftover tobacco into tin boxes, and when they were full, we gave them to our dads. Although Papa was not a heavy smoker, Mama did not like the smell of tobacco. I remember one day, when we were living in Germany after the war, that Mama was upset about something. She grabbed Papa's tin box, opened it, and shook the tobacco out the second-storey window. That was the only time I ever saw Mama so upset that she would do something like that. I never found out what was bothering her. Eventually, Papa gave up the habit a few years later.

On my way home from school one day during the occupation, I saw an old man walking past me. His clothes were tattered and looked like he had been sleeping in them. I turned around to have another look at him, and what caught my attention was a large white star that was sewn onto the back of his shirt. I had seen other people with white stars on their clothes. Eventually, I found out that these were Jewish people who were made to wear the stars so that they could be identified as Jews.

Two houses over from us, there lived a Jewish family. They had a beautiful, all-brick house with very large rooms. We knew them quite well. Their last name was Schiff, and they had two daughters, Zilia and Olga. Olga was my age, and she was one of my friends. The girls' mother would come over every so often to borrow things like sugar, eggs, or kitchen utensils. The family had planned to leave the area before the German occupation, but they hadn't had time to escape. Everything happened so quickly. One day I saw Mr. Schiff walking down our street. He had his pocket watch in his hands, and he was trying to sell it to one of the German soldiers. No doubt the family had run out of money for food. Eventually, we lost sight of the family; they just vanished. Shortly thereafter, a new family moved into the Schiffs' house, and we knew then that the Jewish family had been shipped off, never to be heard from again. The other Jewish families who hadn't escaped before the occupation met the same fate.

One of Mama's sisters, my Aunt Helen, lived with us off and on and was proficient in German and Russian. She was hired by the German forces to be a translator in the city of Zaporizhzhia, on the east shore of the Dniepr River. When she came for a visit on her days off, she would tell my parents of the horrible things she knew were happening to the Jews that were rounded up. Her office was within hearing distance of the place where the soldiers would congregate after returning from a special assignment. There she would hear them joking about the groups of Jews they took out of town in trucks to be lined up and shot in front of freshly dug trenches. They would laugh about how it sounded like watermelons popping when they shot the Jews in the head. My parents knew of some of the things that were going on, but they did not talk about them openly.

During the time that I went to German school, many children had a problem with head lice. I remember a girl in my class who was sitting at the desk in front of me. She had long braids. One day, as I was admiring her braids, I noticed some lice moving through her hair. As lice are easily passed between children, it wasn't long before Mama noticed me scratching my scalp. As soon as she found evidence of hair lice, she rubbed coal oil into my hair in the evening and tied a kerchief tightly around my head. Then she washed my hair the next morning and used a fine-tooth comb to get rid of the dead lice and nits (eggs).

As time went by, we got to know a few of the soldiers that were staying in our garden. Some of them popped in for a visit, and Mama noticed that they would scratch themselves constantly. Upon questioning them, they admitted that they had trouble with body lice. Mama offered to help. She told them to bring their long johns to her. She turned them inside out and ironed the seams where the lice had laid their eggs. The heat killed both the lice and the eggs. Problem solved.

One evening we had two soldiers come for a visit. While the adults were conversing, one of the soldiers reached for me and placed me on his lap. I was a shy child and never liked to sit on anybody's lap, much less a stranger's. I tried to wiggle out of his hold on me, but to no avail. He held me tight with one hand, and he discreetly used the other hand behind my back to slip it into my underwear. No one seemed to be aware of what was going on because German soldiers were known to show kindness to children, quite often openly, and I was not making a sound. I was afraid to say anything because he was a soldier in uniform, and I was just a child. My Aunt Helen, who was visiting, came into the room and noticed there was something wrong with me. My face was flushed, and I looked frightened. She reported the soldier to the commander who was staying in our house. I don't know what the consequences were for that soldier, but we never saw him near our house again. It was years after that event that I learned what a pedophile was.

As winter approached, the German army personnel in our garden moved on to follow their commander to the newly occupied areas. For a while, life in our house became normal again. My parents regained their bedroom, and my father changed jobs. Mama took in sewing, and Grand-mama continued making our meals. I took piano lessons, since we had acquired a piano in recent months. Papa had never had a piano lesson in his life, but he composed a piece of music for Mama, and he played it often, getting better at it every time. Even in his golden years in Canada, he would go to the piano after dinner while Mama was clearing the dishes in the kitchen, and she would hear him play his composition.

Christmas was approaching, and it was the first time in years that we were actually able to celebrate it open-ly. Mama made her specialty, a Napoleon torte, for that occasion. A Napoleon torte is made of five to six layers of pastry filled with vanilla buttercream. It tasted heavenly. In later years, Mama would make it when someone in our family was having a birthday.

In school, we learned the art of calligraphy, and the teacher had all the students in our classroom copy a Christmas poem from the blackboard to give to our par-ents as a Christmas gift. I drew an evergreen branch with a red candle at the bottom of the page, and I was quite proud of the finished product. On Christmas morning, I handed the page to my parents after first reciting the poem for them.

During the German occupation, we lived on ration cards, as food was not plentiful. There was only one food store within walking distance of our house, and there were always lineups when we went shopping. Quite often, Val and I were sent to buy bread. We didn't like having to stand in line, but that was life, so we didn't complain.

For almost two years, life was fairly peaceful. Then, toward the end of September 1943, we got word that the German army was retreating. The Russian army was taking back territory from the Germans. There was no denying that, within a short time, Kichkas would fall into Communist hands again. That was not good news for us because we knew that, if and when the Communists returned, we would be exiled from our hometown and my father would be taken from us.

All people of German descent were told to pack up their belongings and be ready for evacuation to Germany. Although my father was Russian, my mother was of German descent, so my parents worked frantically to pack the things we would be able to take with us. Papa managed to crate up a couple of original paintings that were his prized possessions. He had purchased them from our next-door neighbour who had been shipped off to Siberia before the German occupation. We also took along the two bicycles that my parents owned. I took my doll with me. When we were all packed, Babushka and Djedushka (Grandpa)

"Poohoo" came to say their goodbyes. That was the last time we saw them.

A German army truck showed up. By this time, we did not own any animals other than our dog. We loved him, but we couldn't take him with us. I watched as his leash was being tied to a tree so he would not run away and be shot by a German soldier.

My parents took a final walk through the house that Papa had built with his own hands. The living room ceiling had a beautiful design painted in each corner. Papa had hired an artist to do the work. I had watched that artist lie on his back on a scaffold, with his left hand supporting his right hand, as he used special paint tools to apply the design. There was the newly acquired piano, and a Kroeger clock at one end of the living room. A Kroeger clock looks a lot like a grandfather clock, but without the cabinet. It hangs on the wall and has a pendulum and chains with weights attached to the ends. To wind the clock, the chains must be pulled every twenty-four hours. That was Grandmama's job every night before going to bed. Kroeger clocks were popular in German homes. You could say that there was one in every household. There are still a few of them in Canada, brought by their owners when they fled Russia and then passed down to their children and grandchildren.

There was no point in locking the house. We knew we would never be back. With tears and heavy hearts, my parents turned their backs on our garden and everything that represented life as we knew it. After our possessions were loaded onto the truck, one by one we were helped up, beginning with Grandmama, who was coming with us. The truck took us to the railway station, where we waited with close to a thousand other people for the train that would take us to Germany. Two of my aunts were there as well, with their children. Their husbands had been taken away by the Communists.

The train finally arrived, and to our disappointment, it was not a passenger train, but one consisting of a long row of boxcars. The floor of each car was covered with piles of straw for us to sit or lie on. All the baggage was loaded into the cars first, and then the people climbed up. The cars were full to capacity. I sat close to my Grandmama, holding onto my doll. The German army personnel who were in charge took a long time making sure everyone was accounted for. Finally, the train blew its whistle, the doors of the car were shut, and we began to move. We sat in total darkness. There was an eerie stillness. Now and then, you could hear some whimpering as women gave way to their emotions.

Occasionally, the train stopped because of the air raids, and we were told to run for protection from enemy bombing. When we were hungry, we ate what we had brought along, mostly heavy rye bread with some of the smoked ham that my parents had salted away in a small barrel. We also had a sack of dried fruit. We did not know how long we would be in transit. As it was, it took two weeks to get to the German border. The train stopped every so often so that the people could get out of the cars to relieve themselves. We also had a chamber pot with us, just in case one of us children had to go while the train was moving. We could always tell by the number of times the locomotive whistled whether the train was stopping for a washroom break or for us to get out and scramble for cover from the incoming bombers. If the train stopped in a wooded area, we were to run and hide in the woods. If it stopped in the open, we would just huddle together, close to the ground, until we heard the all-clear signal from the locomotive, which meant we could board the train again. This was a daily routine. We never knew if we would get to our destination safely because of the possibility of sabotaged bridges or railroad tracks. Sometimes the train sat for several hours and waited until the damaged tracks were repaired.

After arriving in Litzmannstadt (now Lodz), Poland, we were put through a cleansing ritual. Everybody had to leave the train and go to a large building. The women and girls were taken to a separate area from the men and boys. We had to undress and put our clothes on a conveyor belt for delousing and bacteria removal. After taking a shower, we were guided into a large gymnasium-type room where everybody was lined up naked against the four walls. We were allowed to keep our shoes/boots on. I was shaking, unsure of whether I was cold or scared of what was to come. The doors flew open, and several German doctors in uniform came in. They slowly went from person to person and looked us over from top to bottom. Not a word was said to us.

After the inspection, we were directed to the area where we had undressed. No one spoke. Needless to say, it took a while for each of us to find our own clothes, which were dusted with white powder. After getting dressed, we waited for our fathers and brothers to join us so that we could board the train together. After the doors were shut and the train began to move, we could hear a low murmur among the adults. No doubt they were sharing their opinions about what had just happened.

Three

Germany: Life in the Refugee Camp

On October 9, 1943, we arrived in Neustadt, West Prussia, near Danzig (Gdansk). It is now part of Poland and has another name. The doors of the boxcars were opened, and all of us, with our belongings, were taken to a refugee camp that was surrounded with barbed wire fencing. There, each family was assigned living quarters in barracks. We had to share our room with two other families. There were six double bunk beds in that one room. They were all lined up along the walls, end to end. The baggage was stashed under the beds or, if there was room, at the end of the beds. We were issued grey horse blankets that were hung from the top bunk beds for privacy, and each family received meal tickets that were collected when we picked up our daily rations.

Passes were issued to the adults who found work outside the camp as well as to the schoolchildren. These passes were checked at the gates when people left or returned to the camp. Washrooms were situated at either end of the camp. There we washed our faces and brushed our teeth. Once a week, we had to stand in line to use the baths. One of the barracks was used as a hospital, and I had to stay there when I came down with the measles.

We settled in quickly. Papa offered his services and became the camp's groundskeeper. We children started school, which was downtown, several kilometres from the camp. At the beginning of class in the morning, when the teacher arrived, we all had to stand up, raise our right arms shoulder-high, and give the "Heil Hitler" salute. We would do the same when we left the class to go home. The teacher talked about Hitler almost every day, telling us how wonderful our "Fuehrer" (leader) was.

Within a few months, makeshift offices were set up on a train. All families had to show up, documents in hand, to be processed and issued passports. Interrogation took a long time, but in the end, everybody was handed German identification papers. A few families, like mine, were not considered pure German due to interracial marriage. Hence our passports were of a different colour than the ones received by families where both spouses were of German descent. That meant my family would not have the same rights and privileges in Germany as the rest of the people. We would be restricted to travelling only to certain areas in Germany.

Discrimination was not foreign to my family. When we lived in Russia, my older brother was often teased by the Russian children he played with for having a "foreign mother" because of her German heritage. Now he experienced the same treatment in Germany because of my father being Russian. Val would stand up to the boys who teased him and would quite often come home with a bleeding nose. Papa had trouble speaking the German language, so no matter how hard he tried, he could not hide his Russian accent. Hitler's philosophy was that the German race was superior to any other, but when Mama married my father, she did not know she was "contaminating" the next generation. Is it any wonder, then, that my parents lived in fear of a future under Hitler's leadership?

While at camp, every family was given a copy of Hitler's book, *Mein Kampf.* I am not sure whether my parents ever read the book, but I remember looking at it and I was impressed by its thickness and by Hitler's picture on the cover. What happened to the book I cannot say, but I know it did not make the list of things that were eventually packed for our quick getaway toward the end of the war.

During the time we lived at the camp, all the boys and girls ten years and up were integrated into the Hitler Youth movement. During the summer months, we were taken as a group on several outings into the woods which surrounded our camp. I must admit I enjoyed those few days of being out in nature, away from the prison-like environment of the camp. Of course, we were indoctrinated into the ways of Hitler's dreams. One of Hitler's songs had these words: "Today Germany belongs to us and tomorrow the whole world will be ours." That song was sung at every one of our get-togethers.

The meals at camp left much to be desired. The portions were small, and there wasn't much meat in any of them. We would still feel hungry after finishing our rations. The women took turns peeling potatoes in the cellar under the camp kitchen. One time when it was Mama's turn, I went with her to help, and I felt sick from the stench of rotten potatoes and the dampness in the cellar.

One summer morning, all the children ten years and up were taken by trucks to a farm to pick kohlrabi. We were cheap labour, but we were doing it "for the Fatherland." We picked all day as the sun beat down on us. No one brought us anything to eat or drink. When we were hungry, we ate some of the kohlrabi that we picked. At the end of the day, before returning to camp, we were served kohlrabi soup. I can say for certain that I have never had kohlrabi since.

Besides the wooden bunk beds, all the barrack walls and ceilings also consisted of wood. Bedbugs loved to hide in the wood crevices. They were almost the size of ladybugs—round, flat, reddish in colour, and fast. They also hid in the ends of the wooden beds. At night, after the lights went off, the bedbugs dropped from the crevices in the ceiling. I slept in an upper bunk bed, so I was very close to the ceiling. If I got bitten before I fell asleep, I would call out to Papa. He would turn the light on, and immediately the bugs would scramble for safety. He always managed to get a few of them by spearing them with a long needle. That caused me to wrinkle my nose, as I am very sensitive to smells, even to this day, and the bed bugs that were speared emitted a peculiar odour.

One day, the ladies in our barrack decided to do something about the bedbug problem. They took all the bunk beds apart and dragged them outside. Then they brought kettles of boiling water from the kitchen and poured it over the wood. That flushed out any bedbugs that were lodged in the crevices. This was the only way we got relief from them for a while.

Mama was one of the many camp women who had to work at an ammunition factory. They were picked up by trucks early in the morning and brought back in the evening. What exactly they did at the factory was not talked about openly. If anybody asked what she did, she had to say she "packaged medication." That was free labour for the country.

One day, we received news that a truckload of clothes and shoes was on its way to our camp for distribution. It caused much excitement among the refugees because the few clothes we had were getting threadbare, and the shoes had seen better days as well. We lined up, and everybody found something to wear. I found a pair of shoes that was just the right size for me. They were made of beautiful, soft leather. The colour reminded me of cocoa, which I had had once or twice in my early years. There was a narrow strap that went across the foot, and it was fastened with a leather-covered button. I had never had such nice shoes before. In the coming days, I overheard the adults talking about the source of the items that had been distributed. Word was that the clothes had belonged to the Jews that were gassed in the concentration camps. This was never talked about openly in the camp, but I remember that Mama was very upset when she heard this, and she couldn't sleep for several nights after that.

Of course, today it is a well-known fact that millions of Jews met their deaths in European concentration camps, and thousands were shot and buried in ravines in Eastern Europe at the hands of the German Wehrmacht. In the Kiev area, all the Jews were rounded up in September 1941 and taken to the ravine named Babi Yar. They were ordered to take their clothes off before going into the huge trench where they were shot to death. The number of them was 100,000. Some of them were not Jews, but high Soviet officials. Who knows what happened to their clothes?

In the summer of 1944, the year after we arrived at the camp, I happened to be one of three girls who were chosen to go to a Hitler Youth camp for a week. I was very excited. Mama packed a few of my things for me, and the three of us set out for the train station. We had been given an address and were told how to get to the camp after leaving the train. It was a hot day, and we were looking forward to getting a drink of cold water after arriving at camp. When the train stopped, we followed the directions given and found that it was a long walk to the camp, which was in the country. We had no trouble finding it, but after arriving there, we didn't see any children or outdoor activities. When we entered the closest building, we only saw two adults stacking chairs and cleaning. They told us the camp was closed by order of the Wehrmacht, as enemy forces were advancing toward that area. Needless to say, we were very disappointed. We were hungry, as we had not eaten since morning, and nobody offered us even a glass of water. We made our way back to the train station and had to wait a couple of hours before finding a train that was going back the way we had come. Consequently, we arrived at our camp late in the evening. In retrospect, I can say it was a good thing we were sent back so quickly. The next day, the Hitler Youth camp area became the battleground between the Germans and their enemies.

In the fall of 1944, as Germany was losing hold of its occupied areas, we started to hear air raids several times a day, and we knew that we were not safe. The camp had no bomb shelters. Every time we heard the air raids in the middle of the night, we would have to leave the camp in groups, head into the woods that surrounded the camp, and stay there until we heard the all-clear signal.

It was during these fall months that all the men in the camp, including my Papa, were drafted into the People's Army to dig trenches on the front lines and do manual work for the army. My parents had decided earlier on that, in case of an emergency, we would go to Dresden to stay with one of Mama's sisters, Aunt Tina, who had been living there with her family since leaving her little farm in Russia.

Before Papa left the camp, he crated up the two paintings and the bicycles that we had brought with us from Russia and shipped them to Dresden. Shortly after that, the rest of the camp people were told by the leadership that we were free to leave for safer parts of Germany. Grandmama had left camp a few months earlier to stay with another one of her daughters, Aunt Anne, who had landed in Poland with her family after escaping the war zone in Russia.

Mama quickly packed our belongings into our only suitcase. It was an evening in January 1945. We had to walk to the railway station, which was a few kilometres from camp. Mama and Val took turns carrying the suitcase. I carried my doll, cradled in one arm, and my younger brother Alex held my other hand. Mama's sister-in-law and her two children also came with us. Mama's youngest sister and her three children, who had arrived at the camp with us from Russia, stayed behind, as she had no one to help her. She hoped the Soviets, after finding out that her husband had been drafted into the Russian army at the beginning of the war, would take pity on her and leave her and the children alone. However, that was not the case. When the camp was invaded by the Soviets, she and her family were repatriated to Russia after all.

It was dark by the time we arrived at the train station. I was tired, and I would have been happy to crawl into my bunk bed, bedbugs and all, and go to sleep. I had no comprehension of the impending danger. There were hundreds of people around us, waiting for a train that would take all of us to safety. It finally arrived, and we found that it was going toward Dresden. When it stopped, everybody ran to get on. There was a lot of pushing and shoving. Mama, seeing that I would not be able to take my doll with me, asked me to leave it behind. So, with quivering lips and a few tears running down my cheeks, I laid it gently on the ground, hoping that someone else would pick it up and give it the love that I had. Then I ran to join my family. All of us made it onto the train. The passenger car was filled to capacity, and we had to stand near the door, squeezed together like sardines. For a while, I stood on only one foot, until someone finally moved over a couple of inches. That is how we travelled on the first night of our journey to Dresden—a journey we didn't know would take three weeks.

Every so often, the train would stop in a city long enough for the Red Cross to hand out pieces of buttered bread and hot drinks to the people on board. At one of the stops, while waiting for a replacement train, we went to the waiting room at the station. The area was packed with wall-to-wall people that, just like the rest of us, were trying to get away from the danger that seemed to be following us and, at times, looked ready to overtake us. Needless to say, every chair was occupied. We huddled together on the floor in one corner, and I fell asleep. Suddenly, I got up and started to walk toward one of the tables where some German soldiers were sitting and drinking out of their flasks. I took a flask right out of a soldier's hand and started to walk away with it. Mama, who had been dozing, saw me. She realized that I was walking in my sleep, and she came running after me. She returned the flask to the soldier and apologized profusely. Then she led me back and sat me down, and I continued to sleep. I had never sleepwalked before, nor have I since. I guess my body was under stress at that time.

When we got on the next available train, we found that the passenger car was full of released prisoners. There was no room for us to sit, so we stood again. Mama told us to keep quiet and not to talk to any of the prisoners, as she was concerned for our safety. They were a rowdy bunch of criminals, and with no security on the train, were capable of anything. We were very relieved when they finally got off the train at one of the stops and we were able to secure some seats before other people crowded into the car.

When the train stopped for the night, the Red Cross guided us to a school gymnasium, where we slept on straw. Morning came too soon. We were still exhausted, but we had to keep going while the trains were still running. We eventually arrived in Dresden after three weeks of interruptions: railway bombings, track repairs, and changing trains.

All seven of us arrived around midnight: my mother with us three children, and my aunt with her two. (This aunt's husband was Mama's oldest brother, who had been taken from his family and sent to Siberia by the Communists. His two older sons were sent away as well.) There we were, on the streets of Dresden in the middle of the night. Where to go from here? We saw a streetcar coming our way. When it stopped, we asked the engineer if he would let us off at a certain street. No streetlights were on for security reasons, so we could not see any street signs. We had to trust the engineer to let us off at the right stop. After dropping us off, he told us which way to turn to get to the right street. With the help of flashlights, we finally found the right address. It was dead quiet around us. Should we ring the doorbell and wake up the neighbourhood? And what if Aunt Tina had moved with her family in the meantime?

Well, it was after midnight, and we had to do something, so we went ahead and rang the doorbell. It took a while before we heard some movement inside the apartment. Then the door opened, and we knew we had come to the right place.

As we exchanged greetings, we found that yet another aunt, my mother's sister Anne, had arrived earlier during the night with her husband, her daughter, and my Grandmama. Just as we were ready to bed down, the doorbell rang again. To our surprise, it was Papa who walked in! He had escaped from the war zone a few days before and found his way to Dresden, where he knew he would find his family. There was great jubilation. My Aunt Tina and her husband had four of their six children living with them, so now there were eighteen people in that small apartment. We were all exhausted and, needless to say, it did not take twelve of us, lined up on the floor, long to fall asleep.

The next morning, Papa went to the Refugee Bureau, where our family was assigned an address for our stay in Dresden. When we arrived at the address, we were sure there had been a mistake because we were standing in front of a beautiful mansion. However, we went to the gate and rang the bell. Out came an old gentleman who introduced himself as Graf (Count) von Siechert. He and his wife were expecting us, as they had been contacted by the Refugee authorities earlier. In those days, even people of nobility were not spared from having to take in refugees. Count von Siechert was eighty years old, but his age did not deter him from taking our suitcase, the only one we had, and carrying it up the wide winding stairway to the rooms assigned to us. My parents and brothers stayed on the second floor, while I was accommodated in a small bedroom on the main level. I couldn't believe my eyes when I opened the door and saw a bed covered with a thick goose down duvet. The room was cold, and the ceramic tile floor did not make it any warmer. However, I was given a hot water bottle, and once I got into bed, I felt like a chick under its mother's wings. That night I had the best sleep I had had in a long time.

The mansion was on a hill overlooking the city of Dresden. In the next few days, my brothers and I had a great time exploring the grounds behind the mansion. There was a path that wound its way up a hill past a small gazebo-type building that was used by a local artist when he came to paint the surrounding landscape during the different seasons of the year. The mansion's furniture was from the Renaissance period. There were portraits on the walls, depictions of royalty connected to the Count and Countess von Siechert. The whole scenario was something out of a fairy-tale book. When we heard the air raids, our family would go into the cellar with the owners of the mansion and stay there until the all-clear signal was heard. That was the only time we were allowed in the cellar. Here again, there was much to see. Literally hundreds of wine bottles of every vintage lined the shelves along the walls.

It was bedtime on the night of February 13, 1945, when we heard the air raids and headed for the cellar. During the day you could clearly see the downtown core of the city of Dresden below, even from the cellar windows. However, at night, everything was in darkness. The streetlights were not on, and all windows were covered in order to deflect the enemy's attention from the city buildings. Suddenly, we heard the hum of the airplanes overhead, and there were many of them.[2] We saw fire falling from the sky. It was as if gasoline were being poured over the city and, in no time, the whole downtown of Dresden was enveloped in flames. We couldn't believe our eyes. Were we sitting in the front row of a horrible movie? Or was this a dream?

The very next day, February 14, the bombers came back to finish the job they had started at night, and history tells us that 35,000 people lost their lives during this attack. There was a road that wound its way past the mansion, and over the following days, we children stood at the gates and watched as trucks loaded with charred bodies drove by. It seemed like a caravan with no end in sight.

We got in touch with my Aunt Tina to see if her family was safe. At that time, her two oldest daughters were living and working in downtown Dresden. She told us that on the night of the first bombing, her daughters ran into a bomb shelter only to find that the building above them had been hit and was in flames. There happened to be a German soldier in the shelter who told them to hold onto

---

[2] Here is a sentence taken from the account of the fiftieth anniversary of the bombing of Dresden, which was published in our local newspaper, The Ottawa Citizen, on Feb.13, 1995: "The flames and devastation were unleashed by 1,083 Allied bombers dropping 3,430 tonnes of explosives on a city centre that had no strategic significance."

his coat tails and run with him. He took them past the burning buildings and somehow managed to bring them to safety.

When I think of that terrible event in history, I am amazed that my family was spared. In retrospect, I know now that we were safe under God's mighty wings of protection.

After the bombing of Dresden, we knew we could not stay there. The word was that the Soviets were advancing toward Dresden, and we certainly did not want to be there when they arrived. My parents made a decision to leave Dresden and continue on to Sonneberg, a city in Thuringia. They had heard that the situation there was still safe. Papa and Val went to the train station to check out the daily schedule. Just before arriving at the station doors, they stumbled over what looked like a small crate lying on uneven ground. Taking a closer look, they recognized the crate that contained Papa's paintings and the two bicycles that he had packed up for Dresden. What a coincidence! The crate had obviously made it to Dresden but was never delivered to my aunt's address.

Dresden's damaged rails had been repaired after the fire, and the trains were on the move again. Papa redirected the crate to Sonneberg. We contacted all three of my aunts who were in Dresden with their families and told them of our plans to leave the city. My Aunt Tina and family did not want to leave. Consequently, they were repatriated to Russia when the Soviets arrived. The other two aunts and their families, who had arrived in Dresden the same night as we had, decided to leave with us. All twelve of us, including Grandmama, met at the train station toward the end of February 1945, and with our belongings, we boarded the train that was bound for Thuringia. The locomotive gave a few short whistles, and slowly we started to move. I pressed my face against the window to see the last of the devastation of Dresden disappear before my eyes. Soon the vegetation changed into a thick forest on both sides of the moving train. We were approaching beautiful Thuringia, well-known for its winter sports. The composer Johann Sebastian Bach spent the first part of his life (1685-1717) in Thuringia. The city of Sonneberg is known for its toy factory, which ships its well-made toys all over the world. There is also a toy museum. Had we arrived there in peacetime, we would have done some sightseeing.

After arriving in Sonneberg, we got off the train and had to make our way up a mountain road to a small town called Neufang, just a few kilometres above the city. It was a fair hike, and we arrived safely with our few worldly possessions. For the first night, we slept in a school gymnasium on straw mattresses. The next day, each of our three families was placed in private houses. My family ended up in a three-storey house that was occupied by three families, one on each floor. We received one room on the top floor that served as a kitchen and bedroom, with a skylight for a window and one room on the second floor.

We found the people of Neufang very friendly. Everywhere you went, you would be greeted with "Gruess Gott!" ("God speed!"). However, within a short time of our arrival, there came a command from the Wehrmacht that the only greeting to be used in that town was "Heil Hitler." It didn't matter whom you met. Even when we went to the store for something, we had to raise the right arm and say, "Heil Hitler" to the storekeepers.

My brothers and I started to attend school. The local stores didn't have much food available, even though we had ration cards. We would go to the store, stand in line, and by the time we got to the counter, they would be sold out of bread or whatever else we needed. Yet the towns-people never seemed to go without. It seemed like the ref-ugees were treated differently from the local people. Sev-eral times, when I was sent to the store, I would pick up a multigrain meal that had the consistency of cornmeal. People bought this to feed their pigs after adding water and cooking it until it became thick. Mama would cook it with onions and whatever vegetables were available, and many times it was the meal of the day.

Word spread that Papa was good at fixing things like small appliances, clocks, and radios. So, the people of Neufang would bring him all kinds of things to fix, and he would be paid with vegetables or a few eggs. Eventu-ally things became so bad that we started to get sick. My brother Val fainted one day because of hunger.

During the last days before Germany capitulated in May 1945, we got news that a warehouse in Sonneberg was giving away all its merchandise. All we had to do was show up. Val was fourteen at that time, and I twelve; we borrowed a wagon from the neighbours and headed down the mountain on the road that would take us to down-town Sonneberg. As soon as we reached the outskirts of the city, the air raids went off, and we scrambled to find a sign that would show us the way to a bomb shelter. We were fortunate in spotting one almost immediately, and we ran as fast as we could, dragging our wagon behind us. We stayed in the shelter until we heard the all-clear signal, and then we couldn't get out of there fast enough to make our way to the warehouse. There were a lot of people all running in the same direction. No doubt they had heard the news about the free giveaway. When we got there, everybody was pushing their way toward the doors, which were closed. Nobody was allowed in. The merchandise was thrown from a platform into the crowd. After we caught several bolts of fabric and bundles of running shoes, we started to make our way back up the mountain. We were just barely out of the city when we heard the air raids again, but there was no bomb shelter in sight. We parked our wagon a bit off the road and crawled under a bush to wait. We could clearly hear airplanes flying above our heads, and I crawled closer to my brother. I felt protected being near him. It seemed like a while before the all-clear signal sounded. We crawled from under the bush and resumed our trek back to our town in the mountains.

The next day, Papa and Val took the loaded cart and started out for the country. They went from farm to farm and exchanged yards of fabric and several pairs of running shoes for food. They were gone three days. Sometimes farmers would put them up in the barn for the night. They returned with small amounts of bacon, eggs, butter, and vegetables. We were overjoyed to have food for the next while. That is how we survived.

When the air raids sounded, we would run into the basement with the rest of the people that lived in the house. During the waiting time in the basement, some of the ladies would keep busy knitting, while the rest of the adults would speculate as to what would happen when the "enemy" arrived in our small town.

Four

The End of the War

One day we heard that American combat troops had entered Sonneberg, and within a few days, on May 8, 1945, the war was over. Subsequently, the U.S. Military Administration was in control of all of Thuringia. That included our town, Neufang.

There were no noticeable changes in the town once the war was over. Life went on as usual. However, my family and all the other refugees in town wondered what would happen to us now. Would the American administration hand us over to the Soviets to be repatriated to the land of our birth? The German population, whose homes were being shared with the refugees, would certainly be glad to have them vacated so they could have their privacy back. It was common knowledge that, if this happened, we would never see our birthplace. Most likely we would be shipped off to an area like the Ural Mountains, as a punishment for having "collaborated" with the Germans.

Soon after the American occupation, we moved to Sonneberg, where the refugees were assigned temporary quarters. We were happy to move into newly built barracks where every family was accommodated in small, two-room apartments. We knew that this was just for a short period of time, until the big issue of Germany's future was settled. After all, they had lost the war; who would take on the administration of a defeated and devastated country? Eventually, the decision was made to divide Germany into four sectors: the United States, Russia, England, and France would each control a part of Germany. We were not sure under whose control we would end up living, but we knew one thing for certain: we would do everything we could to stay away from the iron rule of Communism.

Well, the worst news came. All of Thuringia would be handed over to the Soviets by July 1, 1945. We got together with the relatives who had travelled with us, and several of our other refugee neighbours and made plans to leave Thuringia and move to Bavaria, which was to stay under U.S. administration. We quickly packed our things—even Papa's two paintings made it yet again, along with the two bicycles—and on June 26, 1945, we were picked up by an American forces truck that would take us to the Bavarian border. Or so we thought. Instead, "through a misunderstanding by the driver," we were taken to a Soviet repatriation camp in Coburg, just a few miles short of our desired destination. *How can this be?* This happened to us after we had done all we could to avoid falling into the hands of the Soviets.

At the gates, a Russian officer ordered us to get off the truck with our possessions and move everything a few metres from the gates. This camp was full of refugees.

Several of the buildings were completely filled up, and the rest of the people were camping outside next to their possessions.

My parents started a conversation with some of them and were told that, the day before, a man had committed suicide because he'd refused to be repatriated. The word was that, once you landed in this camp, you couldn't escape repatriation, which was going on daily. Most likely, Papa would be taken from our family and shipped off to Siberia to do hard labour for deserting his country during the war.

We spent the night sleeping outdoors. I doubt that my parents slept a wink that night. The next morning, Papa went to the camp authorities and informed them that our being dropped off at this camp had been a mistake. He told them we were German Dutch refugees on our way to join relatives in Bavaria. He was partly correct: Mama was the one of German Dutch descent. After listening to Papa with his Russian accent, you would think they'd have told him to go back to his family and wait for the camp authorities' next instructions. However, at this point a miracle happened that can only be attributed to God.

"I know the plans I have for you," declares the Lord, *"plans to prosper you and not to harm you, plans to give you hope and a future"* (Jeremiah 29:11). I have learned since then that when God has a plan, no man can change that plan, not even the Communists.

Papa was told to gather his family and the rest of our group, and to go to a certain area where a truck would be waiting to take us to Bavaria. Was this reality, or were we dreaming? Should we trust the Soviets to take us to Bavaria? We decided to take the chance and climbed onto the truck with our baggage in tow. Then we were driven to Bamberg, a beautiful Bavarian city, where we would live for the next two and a half years.

My parents often talked about that "miracle" with their friends. Our documents were a dead giveaway. We were born in Russia, hence according to the Soviets, we were citizens of Russia. Yet here we were, in a safe place and under God's mighty wings of protection. All we know is that our small group was the first, and maybe the only, group of people allowed to leave that horrible camp.

They dropped us off at some barracks in the woods, just outside of Bamberg. During the war, the barracks had been used to house German soldiers. They were just across the road from the American forces' compound and administration buildings. Other refugees besides us were waiting to be assigned living quarters within the city. This area was patrolled by the military police at all times. While we were staying at the barracks, we witnessed several visits from the Red Army. They arrived almost daily, in trucks with Soviet flags attached to them, and used great intimidation to try to persuade the people to go with them. They said Stalin had extended his pardon to everyone who had left Russia during the war, and that our homeland was waiting for us with open arms. Every time they came, we refused their persistent attempts to load us onto their trucks. They would have taken us by force, as they had done with Russian refugees in other parts of Germany, but they knew our area was under American surveillance. Therefore, they had no choice but to leave us alone.

A few days after our arrival in Bamberg, we were assigned one and a half rooms on the second floor of a private residence. The other two families that were travelling with us found accommodations on the same street. We let Grandmama have the half room that was meant to be a future bathroom. It had no bathtub or toilet and was just big enough for her bed and a chair. The rest of us stayed in the other room.

The only bathroom in the house was a powder room on the main floor. It had a sink and a toilet. If we wanted to bathe, we had to go the baths downtown. There, we were issued a number and had to wait until it was called. Next, we found the bathroom with that number on the door. In between baths, the cleaning lady scrubbed the tub for the next person. We had to bring our own soap and towel. There were no hair dryers, so we left the baths with wet hair. However, it felt good to have a hot bath at least once a week.

Another family we had met in the barracks moved into a house next to ours. They had a daughter named Alina who was my age, and she and I became good friends. We rode bicycles, roller-skated together, and explored the woods until school started at the end of summer.

Both Papa and Alina's father got jobs as kitchen helpers at the American army mess. At the end of each workday, the men were allowed to help themselves to the leftovers of the day. That was an answer to prayer, as food was hard to come by in those days, even with the allotment of ration tickets. When Papa came home from work at night, we were all waiting to see what he had in the pail that he carried home. There might be pancakes from the morning's breakfast, a layer of beans with ham from lunch, and then a layer of whatever had been served for supper. Leftover cake was always welcome, as was fresh fruit. Sometimes he brought white bread, a rarity in Germany at that time. Mama would share some of the food with our landlord and his wife.

The walk to work led Papa and his coworker through a wooded area. One day, as they were walking home after work, they saw what looked like a parachute caught in one of the trees. They were able to pull it down and bring it home with them. It was made of pure silk. Mama and Alina's mother took it apart at the seams and dyed all the pieces black. There was enough fabric to make a dress for each of them. A black dress was considered to be elegant wear.

Across the street was an officers club. Val struck up conversations with some of the army personnel. As a result, he started to bring their shirts home for Mama to iron. She did a good job, adding creases where they wanted them. As payment, the soldiers gave us cigarettes, chocolates, and other treats that were hard to come by. Val sold the cigarettes, which brought a very good price on the black market. He made friends with a black officer who came by for a visit every so often. That officer tried to tell us about his family back home in the United States, but conversation was difficult, as none of us could speak much English. However, he was very patient and tried hard to make himself understood. When he saw that Mama, though married, was not wearing a wedding band, he took his own ring off his finger and wanted her to have it because he thought it proper for a married woman to wear one. Mama thanked him, but refused to accept it even though she did not own one.

Some of the officers we met had time off for a short holiday, and they went to Switzerland to explore and do some shopping for their families. One of the officers whose shirts Mama ironed asked if there was anything he could bring back for her, something she could not buy in Germany. She told him she would like a leather handbag and some flowered fabric for a summer dress. When the officer returned a few days later, he brought enough fabric for two dresses and a leather handbag she used for many years afterwards. She wanted to pay him for the items, but he refused to accept any money and told her that ironing his shirts for him was payment enough.

We were amazed at the kindness we were shown by the American forces. This kind of thing would never have happened under Soviet occupation. The Soviet forces were known to plunder the stores as soon as they entered a city, and they also raped German women in celebration of having won the war.

About eight months had passed since we'd left the refugee camp in Neustadt and arrived in Bamberg. We had missed a good part of the school year, and it was time to get back to class again. Alex, who was eight years old, started school nearby. In Germany, after a child finishes grade four, it is up to the parents to decide which school their child should attend, depending on their perception of the child's ability to prepare for a successful academic future. My parents checked out the schools in Bamberg and decided I should attend a "Gymnasium": that is, a school that focuses on academic education and prepares students for university. In order for me to start attending that school, I needed to catch up on one year of Latin language studies. My parents found a tutor who was proficient in that language, and by the time the new school year began, I was on a par with the other students in Latin. English was added the following year.

School started at 8:00 a.m., with recitation of the Lord's Prayer every morning. Most students in the class crossed themselves at the end of the prayer, so I followed suit and did the same. Religious classes had to be attended once a week. The majority of students in my class were of the Roman Catholic persuasion, as were most of the people of Bavaria. There was one Jewish boy who didn't have to stay for religious classes, and he just goofed off during that time. The rest of us "Protestants" had to walk to another school for our religion class. I did not know what "Protestant" meant other than not being Catholic, so I didn't mind being "Protestant" if it meant that I could walk with the other few students to a different location. It was a nice break from sitting in class.

Sometimes, on my way home from school, I would take a shortcut down a country road and then through a park. At times, while walking through the park, I saw some activity going on behind the bushes. There in broad daylight, I would see teenage girls as young as fourteen prostituting themselves with American soldiers for an orange or a chocolate bar.

On one side of the semidetached house where my family stayed, there lived a seventeen-year-old prostitute. She rented the best room of the house. It was facing the street. Every living room in those semidetached houses had a potbellied stove to keep warm in the winter. In the mornings as I left for school, I saw her come outside, usually dressed in a light blue satin negligee, with a pan of ashes in her hand that she disposed of in the front garden. At the same time, an American soldier would leave her door. I felt sorry for her and often wondered whether she had any family.

Just a block down the street lived another prostitute. I thought she wore a lot of makeup. Also, she wore fishnet stockings. In those days you would see only prostitutes wear them. Their American boyfriends showered them with gifts of clothes they bought for them in Swiss shops.

From the time we arrived in Bamberg, my Grandmama was bedridden. She had pain throughout her body and never left her room. The doctor would come to the house and give her strong medication, but it didn't seem to do her much good. I usually saw her in her room after coming home from school, and that's when I would have a little chat with her. On the evening of October 14, 1945, we watched Grandmama take her last breath in her sleep. She was seventy-seven years old. My parents found a pastor to conduct the funeral. Papa made a beautiful wreath of evergreens and very large white mums to be laid on Grandmama's grave.

At the cemetery, there was a small pavilion where Grandmama's casket was kept before burial. There were eleven of us at the funeral: my family of five and the two aunts with their families. As my family left to go to the burial place, I walked up to the casket and took a final look at my beloved Grandmama. Her hair still had quite a bit of black among the grey. It was parted in the middle, with her long braids lying at either side of her body. Her wrinkled face spoke of a hard life, but it also spoke of the great love she had had for her family. She had lived through two wars, a typhoid epidemic, the ravages of the Bolshevik revolution, starvation, the deaths of two infants, and the forceful removal of four sons by Stalin's henchmen. Grandmama never verbalized that she loved me, but I always knew of her love for me, just by the touch of her hand on my head or a quick hug. I had a difficult time looking at her and knowing this would be the last time I would see her. I was trying to stop the tears that were now freely running down my face. I turned and ran out of the pavilion.

When we got to the grave site, the pastor gave a short message of comfort, and Mama, her sister, and sister-in-law sang a German song that spoke of a reunion in heaven.

As the casket was lowered into the grave, Papa placed the wreath on top of it, and we left the site with heavy hearts.

Christmas came, and the five of us had breakfast together. We sang "Silent Night, Holy Night" in parts. Papa had a good voice, but his German words were very sparse. He did a lot of humming in between. I received a pair of slippers that Mama had made for me. They were embroidered with colourful flowers. My brothers also received small presents. That was the extent of our Christmas celebrations that year.

In the spring of 1946, my Aunt Helen arrived. We had not heard from her for two years. She found us through the Red Cross organization. Many families were brought together with the help of the Red Cross. Now, with Grandmama gone, my parents used the small room as their bedroom, while my two brothers slept on the bunk beds that were in the large room. The landlord allowed us to use another room in the house which is where my Aunt Helen moved in with her suitcase and guitar, and she and I shared a bed.

Aunt Helen was ten years older than Mama, and although she'd never had any children, the two of us got along very well. She treated me just as if I were her own daughter. She and both her sisters, Mama and Aunt Anne, were quite musical. All three played the guitar and loved to sing. Hardly a week would go by without the three of them getting together on a weekend for coffee and music. This was the first time in years. Through the war years, there hadn't been much singing going on in any household. Now, slowly, there appeared a glimmer of hope on the horizon for the people who had survived the horrors of war. Restaurants that had been closed during the war opened for business again. People started to have an interest in life again.

After my thirteenth birthday, I joined a ballet class that ran two evenings a week in my school building. It became the highlight of the week for me. I loved it and pursued ballet earnestly for two years.

A few months after Grandmama's passing, my parents became interested in spiritual things. Word spread that a Baptist church was forming in Bamberg. We consulted with all three aunts and their families and decided to try it out. We met in an old synagogue that was purchased from the city and given a few renovations. Two services were conducted every Sunday. The first service was in the morning, and it was in German. That is the one my family attended. The second service was in the afternoon, and it was in Ukrainian. We made some wonderful friends at that church, and we stayed in touch with them until we left for Canada. Papa, Val, and Aunt Helen came to faith in Christ there and were baptized there as well. Mama had become a Christian when she was a teenager, and now she rededicated her life to God. As far as I was concerned, I needed time to get all things spiritual sorted out.

Across the street from where we lived, behind the officers club, was a soccer stadium on one side of the street and a field for parking bicycles on the other. During a soccer game, there was a sea of bicycles parked there, and

I often wondered how anybody would be able to find theirs after the game. Besides buses, bicycles were the main means of travel in Bamberg. Everybody used bicycles. Our landlord's wife was pregnant during the time we stayed in their house, and she travelled by bike right up until the time she gave birth. During the weekends, my friend Alina and I would take our fathers' bicycles and ride them all around the stadium. We had a little competition going as to who could ride the longest without holding on to the handlebars.

One day, we watched as hundreds of German prisoners of war were marched onto the soccer field. They were to stay there until decisions were made about what to do with them. This took several days. Fortunately, the weather was cooperating, so some of them took to playing soccer while the others just sat on the ground and rested—all under the watchful eyes of American guards. Mama, upon hearing about them and feeling sorry for their situation, made a huge pot of soup with ingredients that Papa had brought home from work. Then she put the soup into a pail and made her way to the soccer field. She parked herself near the fence and ladled soup into the caps that the prisoners of war passed through the fence. They would drink the soup out of their caps. Of course, it wasn't very long before she was noticed by the American guards, who persuaded her that what she was doing was not a good idea, and that she should take her pail and leave. But that was my Mama: she didn't care what nationality the prisoners were; she just cared for humanity in need.

A little beyond the stadium was an outdoor roller-skating rink. I did not own any roller skates myself, so I would borrow a pair from a girl who lived down the street. She was an excellent skater. It took a few knee scrapes before I got the hang of it, but eventually I caught on and thought I was pretty good at it. The rink was surrounded by woods. Val and I used to go there to look for mushrooms. We knew which were good for eating, and we would often bring a basket full of them home. Mama fried them in butter. That's where I developed a taste for mushrooms. Not far from the end of our street was the forest. We would go there to look for blueberries. One day, we came upon the body of a dead man, lying under a tree with his cane hanging from a branch above. On the way home, we stopped at the first house we came across and reported what we had seen. In no time, we saw an ambulance and a police car heading that direction. We never heard who the dead person was or what had happened to him.

During the time we stayed in Bamberg, we were no longer called refugees, but DPs (Displaced Persons) or *Heimatlose* (people without a country). We received several parcels from the U.S., as did many other DPs. Each parcel was marked GIFT in big letters. One time, when Papa went to pick up a parcel at a postal depot, the clerk who looked after Papa asked what he was going to do with it. The word *gift* in German means "poison." We had a laugh when Papa came home and told us about it. The parcels would sometimes contain clothing items, but the rest would be Crisco, canned goods, chocolate bars, and hygienic products. Crisco was a favourite item to barter with. When one of us needed a new pair of shoes, my parents would take Crisco with them to the shoe store. Shoes were never available, even if you had the money, until the store clerk saw the Crisco; then he would suddenly remember there was still a pair in the back room. Shortening was hard to find in the stores right after the war, so bribery was the way one got things that were not available otherwise.

When I went for tennis lessons, Mama would send a lunch for the instructor along with me. He preferred food to money.

Several theatres that had been closed during the last few months of the war opened their doors for business, and people streamed to them. As in most movie theatres, the newsreel would come before the movie. They showed a lot of the Nürnberg trials, where the Nazis were being tried for the atrocities committed against the Jews during the war. The city of Nürnberg was just a few hours' travel time from where we lived in Bamberg. The newsreel footage showed stockpiles of human hair and storerooms of gold jewellery and gold teeth. All of this came from the Jews who had been killed in the concentration camps. The average German had no idea this kind of thing had been going on during the war, and they were appalled when they saw the newsreels, as were the rest of us.

Bamberg is a city built on seven hills. A year after Aunt Helen joined the family, we found bigger living quarters in a former convent on one of those hills. It had been converted into several apartments and had its own court-yard. It was safe for my brother Alex to play there with the children from the other apartments of the convent. It was built right next door to the *Neue Residenz* (New Residence), a palace that at one time had been inhabited by the prince bishops of the Roman Catholic Church and is now a tourist attraction. It is surrounded with a beautiful rose garden. My family toured this place when we lived next door to it. On my way to school, I would walk down the sloping cobblestone square past the *Dom*, a four-spired cathedral. In the opposite direction, going up the hill, sat the residence of the Roman Catholic Cardinal. Several times a year, religious parades came from that direction, and on those occasions the Bavarian people wore colour-ful ethnic clothes like *dirndls* for the ladies and *lederhosen* (leather shorts) and hats for the men. They carried icons in honour of the Virgin Mary and other Catholic saints.

In this new neighbourhood, Alex attended school, and Val started his first year of teachers college. On his days off, he took pictures of old churches, monuments, castles, and anything else that was of historical significance. He was a very good photographer.

Our landlady was an old spinster who lived with her brother, a retired doctor. We occupied two large rooms. The larger room served as living room by day and a bed-room by night. It had a huge four-poster bed that my parents slept in and a couple of army cots for my two brothers. At one end of the room was a beautiful antique couch and two matching chairs with hand-carved wooden roses all across the top. The other room served as a kitchen, and it also had a double bed that my Aunt Helen and I shared. Occasionally, a travelling missionary would be invited to speak at the Baptist church on a Sunday, and my parents would put him up for the night in the bedroom they shared with my two brothers. Mama would string a curtain between the beds so the missionary would have some privacy. In the mornings, we would have to take turns using the one bathroom we shared with the landlady and her doctor brother.

The U.S. soldiers were known to the local people as "Amis," short for "Americans." After we moved to this new address, Papa asked to be transferred to another army unit so he would not have to travel across town to get to work. One day, after I had taken a message to Papa and was passing the guarded gates on the street, I encountered some teenagers loitering around the area. When they saw me coming through the gates, they started to harass me with a little German ditty. Translated into English, it does not rhyme, but these are the words: "Ami, Ami, Ami my honey, come and jump into my mattress with me." They thought I was a prostitute. I was only thirteen years old at the time, and I felt humiliated.

Sometime during my third year at the Gymnasium, I came home with head lice, most likely caught from other children. It was the worst kind. My scalp was always itchy. For a while, I would spread out a newspaper page on the table and comb my hair over it with a fine comb we called a louse comb, killing the lice as they fell onto the paper.

After a while, when the problem became worse, I would go into the bathroom, comb my hair over the toilet, and keep flushing the lice down. It was such a relief when, with the help of some special products, I finally got rid of that problem.

After the war, the local theatres imported American movies with German subtitles. I had a stack of programs from movies I had attended. I knew all my favourite actors by name, and I would dream about them at night. I loved the happy endings of the movies, and I always hoped that maybe my life would have a happy ending to it as well. Then reality would set in, with its daily hardships, and it would dash my hopes to pieces.

One day, we received a parcel from the U.S. In it was the return address of the people who had sent it, along with a little note. Aunt Helen knew more English than any of us, so she wrote a letter to the dear people and thanked them for their generosity. We got a reply from an Amish spinster from Bally, Pennsylvania. Her name was Lizzy Gehman, and she sent a picture of herself as well as her two single brothers. In the picture, she wore her little white bonnet, and her brothers had long beards and wore hats. At one point, our beneficiaries asked for a picture of our family. All six of us went to a photo studio and had our family picture taken. Eventually, the Amish family offered to sponsor our family if and when the doors opened for U.S. immigration.

Needless to say, we were overjoyed at the prospect of starting a new life in America. That's where the wonderful movies with the happy endings came from. I started to dream again. Life in America would be beautiful. I would have my own bedroom, with an easy chair by my bed and a bowl of fresh fruit on a little table beside it. I would wear clothes just like the ones worn by American girls so I would fit right into American society, and of course, I would speak English.

In the spring of 1948, we were informed that doors were opening up for immigration to Canada and the U.S. Mennonite representatives from both countries were coming to Germany to process those refugees who wanted to emigrate. They were specifically interested in people of Mennonite background who had left their homes during the war, people who were looking to start life in a new homeland. Offices were set up in Backnang, a city about a half-hour drive from Stuttgart, where the head office was located. My family qualified because Mama was of Mennonite background. However, for processing, we had to move from Bamberg to Backnang, in the state of Baden-Württemberg. It took about three hours to get there by car. There was a camp set up to hold the people who had applied for emigration.

Papa got busy packing our belongings, including the crate with his two paintings. My brothers and I had to temporarily put our education on hold.

Rita's parents: Maria and Sergey Tkatschow

Rita's family picture, with Aunt Helen on far right

Rita's passport picture

Aunt Helen, Rita's Mom (Maria),
and Aunt Anne in Bamberg, Germany

Refugee resettlement camp in Backnang, Germany

Girls' sewing class in resettlement camp,
organized by Rita's Mom (background)

Rita's father packed the family baggage for U.S. emigration which did not happen

Rita on the General J.H. McRae, *heading for Canada*

Rita's parents with Alex—coffee time in their Winnipeg apartment. The only part that's left of the German coffee set is the coffee pot, minus the lid.

Get-together in the small kitchen/living room of our apartment, just a few months after our arrival in Canada.
Left to right: Helene Sigrid Schulz, Wilhelm (Bill) Unruh, Peter Kasper at the top, Val in the middle, with Maria Kasper on his knee, and Rita in top right corner.

The ad for the mission that Rita and Val attended during their first year in Canada. This is where Rita decided to follow Jesus.

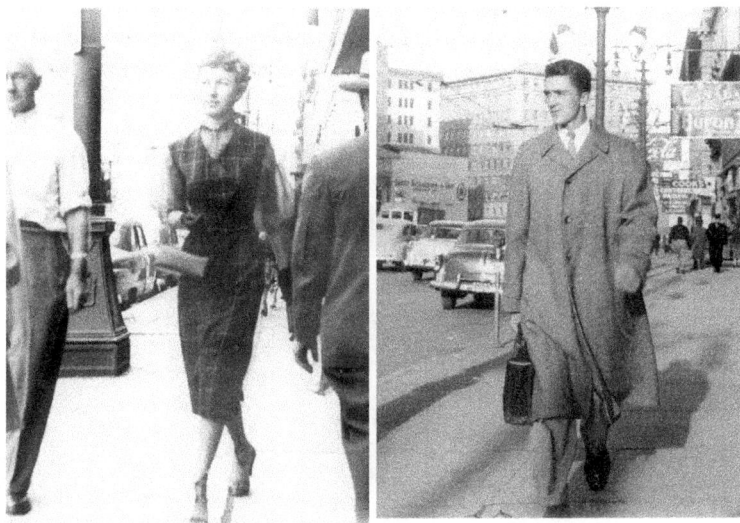

Photos taken by a street photographer on Portage and Main in Winnipeg. Both Rita and Sam (engaged) returning from a day at the office.

Rita and Sam's wedding

25th Wedding Anniversary

Sam and Rita with their children:
Melody, Sam Jr., and Anita

40th Wedding Anniversary

Is there anything better than to play golf on a sunny day?

Rita with granddaughter Nathalie

Rita in her garden with grandsons Jordan and Patrick

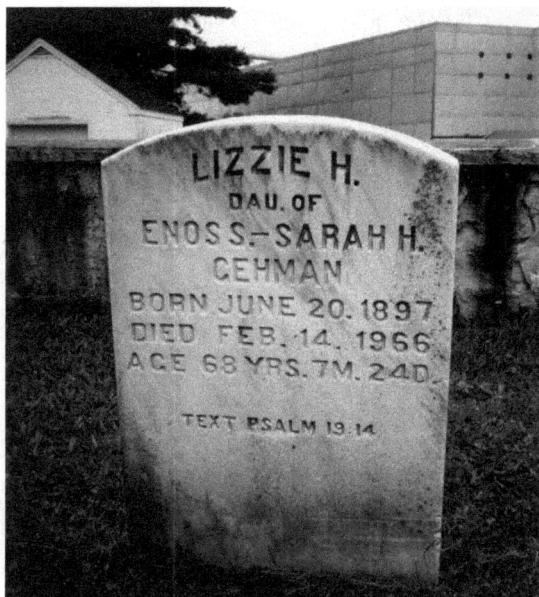

LIZZIE H.
DAU. OF
ENOS S.–SARAH H.
GEHMAN
BORN JUNE 20. 1897
DIED FEB. 14. 1966
AGE 68 YRS. 7M. 24D.

TEXT PSALM 19:14

Lizzie Gehman's grave monument

Rita and Sam caught on camera – tsk tsk!

50th Wedding Anniversary with grandchildren Jordan, Patrick, and Nathalie

Family celebrating Christmas. Top middle: Sam and Rita.
Bottom middle: daughter Anita and Matthew Weston.
Left side: Son Sam Jr. and Gillian
with children Patrick and Nathalie.
Right side: Daughter Melody and Chris Purdy
with married son Jordan and Catherine.

Five

Life in Backnang

There were two resettlement camps set up in Backnang. One consisted of eight barracks that had been occupied by German soldiers during the war, and the other was a vacant factory that had been shut down during the war. When we arrived at the camp, we were assigned a small space in the corner of one of the barracks. There were windows all along the two outer walls of the building, and we were lucky to have one in our space because people whose bunk beds were in the middle row had no windows. Their light came from the bulbs hanging from the ceiling. The space my family occupied was big enough for three double bunk beds surrounded with horse blankets for privacy, and a table with a bench on either side. Lights went off at 11:00 p.m. I slept on one of the upper bunk beds, from which I could see into the surrounding private spaces. At night, when it was quiet, I could also hear the whispering in the neighbouring beds. I would cover my head whenever disagreeable odours wafted up to my level.

In the morning, to brush our teeth and wash our faces, we had to line up at another barrack that had long troughs with water taps every couple of feet. To use the toilets, we walked to the opposite end of the camp to a small outhouse building. One end was for women, and the other was for men. On the women's side were six toilets. They were not the flushing kind. There were also no water taps to wash your hands. I always hurried out of there because of the smell. There were no facilities in the camp for a bath, so we had to go downtown to the baths. For a small amount of money and a wait in line, we came out feeling great after a good soak in the tub.

Our meals were prepared at the camp kitchen. We had to bring our own containers, into which the food was measured out for each person. Then we would take it back to our barrack and eat at the table in our space.

Most of the men at camp found work in the city, and the children were sent to school. Alex attended school within walking distance of the barracks. I attended a high school that offered English instead of Latin. Some of the other subjects that I had not taken before were typing, home economics, and physical education. I was very happy at that school, and I did quite well in all my subjects. My classroom teacher was an older gentleman by the name of Mr. Weber. He made English a fun subject. He also taught the basics of electrical appliances, and because I caught on very quickly in that subject, he and I got along quite well. He was quite strict. Every Monday morning, before class started, we had to attend a weekly church service just for students. The church was within walking distance of the school. He was there early, and his eagle eye made the rounds to see who was missing. You had to have a valid reason for being absent.

Val did not attend school while at camp, but he started a photo studio with his friend, Fred, whom we met when we arrived at the camp. The camp administration allotted Val and Fred two rooms in one of the barracks. One of the rooms was used as a dark room to develop the pictures they took. Besides photographing landscapes and historic buildings, they also did portraits for the people who stayed at the camp. It was a hobby for them, but they also earned some money.

After school and on weekends, I would join Val, Fred, and some of the other young people of the camp in a game of table tennis. I loved the game, and the competition became quite serious among us. During the stay there, we took part in several social outings. Stuttgart was a beautiful city to explore, and it was only thirty kilometres from Backnang, so it didn't take long to get there by train. Val always made sure he had a girl to take with him on these trips. That left me in the care of Fred—who was nineteen, while I was only fifteen—but I never was uneasy in his company because he was a real gentleman.

Mama, Val, and I joined the camp choir after our arrival at the camp, and that was my introduction to choral music. Music was a part of my life for the next fifty-five years.

With the war behind them and the possibility of a new life ahead in either the U.S. or Canada, people in the camp didn't mind living like sardines while their papers were being processed for emigration. It took several months.

While the husbands were at work, their wives got together and started a sewing club. On weekends, Mama and Val taught Sunday School to the children. During the week, Mama led a children's choir to keep them busy when they were not in school, as well as a girls' sewing class and an acting class.

In the fall, a group of people were ready to leave for Canada. Among them were Mama's youngest brother Uncle Julius, Aunt Anne and her family, and Aunt Helen. My longtime friend, Alina, who had come to the camp with her parents, was leaving as well. Anybody that had special ties to my family was leaving, even my friend, Fred, who was a lot of fun to be with, and his parents. As we said our goodbyes, I tried to look happy, but inside my heart was aching. As the train pulled away, a feeling of despair came over me: everybody who had meant anything in my life was now gone.

My family, too, was anxious to leave, and we were waiting for the go-ahead from the American consul because our desire was to go to the United States. In those days, only healthy people were accepted for American immigration. When our family went for a health check, Val's X-rays showed some shadows on his lungs because he had suffered from pleurisy during the previous year. That was cause enough to refuse our entry into the United States. My parents did not give up easily. They decided to separate the family, if permitted: Papa, Alex, and I would leave as soon as possible. Mama and Val would follow us as soon as Val's lung shadows cleared up.

The next spring, in 1949, Papa packed up some of our belongings, including the two paintings that had made their way to Germany. The three of us headed to another resettlement camp in Grohn, Saxony. From here, if we were accepted, we would make our way to Bremerhaven for the ocean voyage to the U.S. and then to Bally, Pennsylvania, where our sponsors, the Amish family, were waiting for us.

Upon arriving at the camp, Papa and Alex were accommodated in the men's multifloor barracks, and a space was found for me in the women-and-children's section of the camp. During the two months we were there, we were given small jobs to keep us busy. Papa helped out in the kitchen; Alex, who was twelve years old, worked at the YMCA; and I, having reached the ripe old age of sixteen, was given a typing job at the U.S. Consulate's camp office. All of us were paid a small amount of money that we could spend on extras.

The camp was under U.S. authority, and every morning, I heard the American anthem played when the flag was raised. I loved that sound, and I looked forward to the time when it would become my national anthem. Every so often, a list would be published of the people that had been approved for immigration to the U.S. The ladies of that group would receive a farewell gift of a drawstring shoe bag filled with all kinds of makeup. I watched as these were being distributed, and although I did not wear any makeup myself, I hoped I, too, would get one soon. But this was not to be. *"In their hearts humans plan their course, but the Lord establishes their steps"* (Proverbs 16:9).

As the days went by and our names did not appear on any of the emigration lists, I took it upon myself to see the American consul for whom I was working. Even though my English was poor, he understood me and checked into our status. He told me that our visa was denied on the grounds that they did not like to separate families. That meant we had to return to Backnang, where Mama and Val were waiting for the news that we had left Germany.

Upon our return, my parents decided that, if we were not allowed entry into the U.S., we would apply for entry into Canada. Papa was quite anxious to leave Germany because he was always afraid that Stalin would eventually find us and that we would be repatriated to Russia. Stalin's belief was that, if we were born there, we were citizens of that country and belonged there. We let our benefactors in Pennsylvania know that we'd been denied entry into the U.S. and then began making plans to leave for Canada.

For a while, life went back to what it was before the three of us had gone to Grohn. It was summer. School was out. There was a youth camp being built in a wooded area outside of Stuttgart. Some young people at the camp were approached to give a couple weeks to this project. There were six of us who volunteered. There was already one building on the grounds that housed the volunteers for the summer. The food was good and plenty, and we worked hard lugging bricks, making cement, and assisting the construction crew where needed. There was also time for relaxation. One night, we went to hear the Red Army chorus give a concert in Stuttgart. They had come all the way from Russia. I knew many of the songs they sang, so it was a very special night for me. On the weekend, we travelled on the back of a U.S. army truck to see Liechtenstein, a beautiful small principality bordered by Switzerland and Austria. It is one of the smallest countries in the world, measuring twenty-five kilometres in length and six kilometres in width. The head of state is the Prince of Liechtenstein, who is very wealthy.

Toward the end of summer 1949, we were advised that we had to move to Gronau, Westphalia, for the final processing before leaving for Canada. Once again, schooling was set aside, Papa did the packing, and his crated paintings went with us yet again. There were many other families from both of the camps in Backnang whose names were on the emigration list, and we all boarded the U.S. trucks that had been provided to take us to Gronau.

When we arrived at our destination, we were accommodated in a huge building that was already three-quarters full of DPs. The rest of us filled up the last quarter. There were no separate rooms; it was all one huge room. Horse blankets were handed out again to make dividers between the bunk beds. Again, I had the top bunk bed, from which I had a view of the whole camp population.

The International Refugee Organization had a complex of emigration offices established downtown, and I, with my typing skills, made myself available to work for them.

There were many music lovers among the camp inhabitants, and it was not long before a choir was formed. Mama, Val, and I signed up, and weekly practices began almost immediately. With all the gloom around us, singing in the choir was like sunshine after a stormy day. Church meetings were held on Sundays, a few blocks from the camp, and that is where the choir performed.

In Germany, people are used to walking everywhere, and that was our mode of transportation. One Sunday, on the way to church, we walked by a store that had beautiful things on display in the window. Mama saw a china coffee set that appealed to her. It was white, with tiny indigo-blue flowers. The next day, we went back to the store, and Mama purchased it. I am sure that when Papa saw it, he probably wondered how he could pack it so it would arrive intact at our destination in Canada. It arrived with not a piece broken, and Mama used the set for many years to serve coffee and cake to family and friends. The only piece that's left of the set now is the coffee pot, which I inherited, minus the lid.

The city of Gronau is close to the border of the Netherlands. There is a place called Enschede on the Dutch side of the border, and our choir presented a concert there one evening for seniors. All the residents enjoyed the music, and for us choir members, it was a nice outing.

Besides showing up at the offices to fill out forms and attend health examinations, all women had to take turns helping in the kitchen or cleaning the washrooms. I hated that part, particularly having to clean the men's washrooms. It made me nauseated just to walk in there.

Christmas came and went, and we celebrated several birthdays. On February 1, we celebrated two birthdays:

Mama turned forty-three, and Alex turned thirteen. My seventeenth birthday was in March, and two of my best childhood girlfriends, Martha and Hertha, who were also in Gronau with us, wished me a happy birthday with a bouquet of flowers and a card that I still have to this day. I wish there had been a birthday cake, but there was none.

Six

Oh Canada, Here We Come!

On the 9th of April, 1950, we were advised that a Canadian sponsor had been found for us. It was a farming family somewhere in Manitoba, outside of Winnipeg. We had to sign a paper stating that four of our family—my parents, Val, and I—would commit to working on the farm for one year. My younger brother, Alex, would be going to school. The last of our papers were finalized, and on April 12, 1950, we arrived at Bremerhaven, where at 3:00 p.m., we boarded a U.S. ship, the USS *General J. H. McRae*. She would take us to our new homeland, to a future we did not know but that we were sure would be better than the past. There were nine hundred immigrants going to the U.S. and three hundred going to Canada.

As the boat moved away from shore, we stood on the upper deck with many of the passengers and waved Germany good-bye. We heard the call for supper and headed to the mess hall. Oh, was the goulash ever good, and there was plenty of it! Shortly after supper, the boat started to rock fiercely. We were heading into a storm. People started to run for the washrooms. When I got to the women's washroom, not one stall was available. They were all occupied, with people throwing up everywhere. I made it to one of the available sinks and noticed that it was plugged up like the rest of them. Seeing that made me twice as sick, but I must say I felt better when I left the washroom. I felt sorry for those who had to clean up all that mess.

As the days went by, Papa, Val, and I volunteered to do small jobs on board. I helped out at the nursing station and made good friends with two nurses from New Orleans. They showed me pictures of their yearly Mardi Gras parades and celebrations, and we kept in touch for about a year after that. They tried to set me up with the U.S. military chaplain who worked on board, a man in his early thirties from New York. He was a nice gentleman, but I was not interested.

For my help at the nursing station, I received coupons that I could trade for merchandise in the ship's store. I was thrilled to find a pair of black silk stockings to wear with the purple dress Mama had bought me before we left for Canada. The dress had a full skirt and a wide belt that made my waistline look small, and I felt the silk stockings would complete the outfit. When I handed my coupons in at the counter of the ship's store, the two young men that looked after me told me I was too young to wear black. They suggested other things they thought would look good on me, but I was not interested in anything but black stockings, which I had wanted for a long time but could not find in any store in Germany. So, I was happy when I walked away with my black stockings in hand.

Many of us were on deck when we passed the White Cliffs of Dover. Mama was seasick during most of the voyage and spent much of her time on deck wrapped in blankets, with Alex keeping her company. When the ship rocked, it was hard getting from one end of the interior to the other because one minute you felt glued to the floor, and the next you found yourself running forward. There was a daily news bulletin produced right on the boat, so we got all the up-to-date world news. Someone on the ship was good at drawing, so there would always be a comic strip of the day depicting a daily boat situation—like some sick person throwing up over the deck's rail. The heading would read, "Feeding the fish."

On April 21, 1950, nine days after we left Bremen, we saw the Statue of Liberty as the ship docked in New York Harbor to unload the U.S.-bound DPs. How I wished it was my family getting off the boat onto American soil. It was because we had only known American soldiers and American people who had been kind to us in Germany following the war. I was envious of the people who were leaving the boat, and it felt like my dream of becoming an American was vanishing right in front of my eyes. We did not know any Canadians and had no idea what to expect in Canada.

Our ship continued on to Halifax, and there, at 8:00 a.m., we arrived at Pier 21. By the time we disembarked, it was 10:15 a.m. We had to go through security and present ourselves to the examining officer. There we received the news that the farming family in Manitoba who had originally offered to sponsor our family had had a change of heart and backed out of their commitment. Now we had a dilemma. We could not leave Pier 21 until we found another Canadian sponsor. Mama had a brother in B.C. who had immigrated to Canada in 1927 to escape the Communist regime. He was contacted, and although he and his wife had five children, he agreed to sponsor our family. Now that we had a sponsor, we decided to stop in Winnipeg, where Mama's two sisters and brother had arrived two years earlier.

We were escorted onto a train that was heading west at 4:00 p.m. Before the train left, we had just enough time to cross the street to a convenience store, where we picked up a few groceries to make some sandwiches. After we were settled in one of the train cars, Val and I took a walk the length of the train just to look around. As we walked through the dining car, a gentleman who was just sitting down for dinner struck up a conversation with us and asked where we came from and where we were going. Then he invited both of us to join him for dinner. We must have looked hungry. We declined, but during the course of our conversation with him, we found out he was a member of Parliament. It was a memorable occasion for Val and me, one that we often talked about later in life.

It was the evening of the following day when we arrived in Winnipeg. Mama's sisters, Aunt Anne and Aunt Helen, and her youngest brother, Julius, came to welcome us at the train station. Then we were taken to Aunt Anne's place, where we stayed for a few days. During this time, we decided to stay in Winnipeg rather than going on to B.C.

When we arrived in Winnipeg, we had no money whatsoever, so we had to find jobs in a hurry. Papa found work as a plumber. His pay was twenty-five dollars a week. Val found work at a photo studio in the Eaton's department store. I found a temporary job in a sewing factory. My pay was seventeen dollars per week. The supervisor lady there made sure I gave one hundred percent to work. I was not allowed to stop and talk to anybody, and when I went for a washroom break, she would make sure I saw her look at the clock so I would know she was timing me. It certainly was not a pleasant place to work. I took the streetcar to work every morning. The fare was five cents one way. After work, I walked home in order to save money.

We found a place for rent and set up a budget for daily necessities, city travel, and a monthly sum to pay off the cross-country journey. It had been paid for by the Mennonite Central Committee, the organization that was responsible for getting us to Canada. There was very little money left for any extras.

After working in the sewing factory just a few weeks, I found work at the Eaton's mail order warehouse. It was located downtown, right next to the Eaton's department store where Val worked. There, the pay was better, and the work was more relaxed. Nobody looked over my shoulder. I made a new friend there, who was also a recent immigrant. Her name was Lucy. In her spare time, she was studying voice. She had a gorgeous coloratura soprano voice, and occasionally, she would sing on a local radio program. Her goal was to become an opera singer. I was very sad when, one day, she announced that she and her family were going back to Austria, where they had come from, because her mother was suffering from cancer and wanted to die in her own homeland.

My family attended the Mennonite church that was about two blocks from where we lived. The services were in the German language. Val and I joined the choir. We got to know a lot of people. My parents also met families whom they had known in Russia.

Summertime was nearing, and we needed some new clothes. We had saved a little bit of money and were able to buy something new for everybody in the family. I bought myself a beige-coloured summer suit for under ten dollars, a pair of pale-yellow sandals for $2.98, a matching purse for $1.98, and a daisy corsage to pin on the lapel of my suit. A pair of nylon gloves completed the outfit. Wow! I was ready to go out.

We were amazed at the abundance of goods we saw in the Canadian stores. Going to Eaton's bargain basement store was like stepping into wonderland. There you could find anything you wanted, and the new immigrants loved to shop there. It covered an area of several thousand square feet, and the clerks were very courteous and seemed to understand the broken English of the new immigrants. We heard about an immigrant lady sending her husband to buy some elastic for her sewing project. When he arrived at the store, he could not find the sewing notions area, nor did he know the English name for elastic. When he was approached by a clerk, while using his hands for emphasis, he said that he needed some "she comes, she goes, she comes, she goes" for his wife. The clerk had no trouble understanding him, and she took him immediately to the notions counter and showed him the place where the elastic was.

In the fall of 1950, the year that we arrived in Canada, I attended a special mission sponsored by the churches of Winnipeg. It was held in the Winnipeg Auditorium and lasted for three weeks. The speaker was Stephen F. Olford, an evangelist from England. I attended most nights, and my heart felt deeply moved by the messages that I heard. I realized that, even though I had not committed any crimes during my short life, nor did I consider myself evil, I was not good enough to meet a holy God without having my sins forgiven. The Bible says that all have sinned and come short of the glory of God and that Jesus, God's Son, paid the penalty for our sins on the cross. Jesus said: *I am the way and the truth and the life. No one comes to the Father except through me* (John 14:6).

At the very last meeting of the mission, I accepted Jesus Christ as my Saviour. I was at peace with God. Now I began to understand that God had a plan for my life. In retrospect, I could see how God had protected me from harm during the past seventeen years of my life. This is when my spiritual journey began.

In the evenings, before going to bed, I would listen to Billy Graham's messages on the radio. Television was not yet available in Canada. Christmas came, and it was very special to me because, for the first time, I appreciated the true meaning of Jesus' birth and the reason for his coming to this earth. I was so glad to know that he came for me, too.

To improve my English, I read anything I could get my hands on. Early in the new year, I applied for a job where I could use my typing skills. As a result, I was hired by a wholesale company to type the bills of lading for the shipping department. I got to know all the girls who were working in the main office when we met for coffee, and I made friends with them. After a few months, I was asked if I would like to work alongside the vice president's secretary. She had a big workload and needed help. I accepted, and my salary was increased. She did all the correspondence for the VP and was also the receptionist. I typed the master copies for the weekly circular ads. Sometimes I would sketch pictures of the specials on the front page. I was not all that artistically inclined, but I was able to do the simple ones. Our company sold dry goods, hardware, furnishings, and small appliances to small-town general stores across rural Manitoba, Saskatchewan, and Alberta. When the secretary I worked for became pregnant, she handed in her notice. I was surprised when they offered me her job. My English had improved to the point that I rarely made spelling mistakes when typing for the VP of the company. I was given a helper who was put in charge of the weekly circular ads.

At one point during my employment with the whole-sale company, I felt that if I wanted to advance in any job,

I would need to go back to school. I thought of joining the Air Force or the Navy. My idea was to get an education and earn an income at the same time. I applied at the local recruiting office but went away disappointed. They told me to come back after I became a Canadian citizen. During that time, you had to reside in Canada for five years before applying for Canadian citizenship, and I would have to wait another two years. So, I decided to stay with the job that I had and leave the future in God's hands.

Eventually, Val and I invested in a used two-seater convertible MG car. He taught me to drive, and we took turns using it. Our arrangement worked out well. We had a lot of fun driving with the top down when the weather was nice. He drove it one week, and I the next. Eventually, a job opportunity opened up for him in Vancouver, so he loaded the car with his belongings and drove it all the way to Vancouver, where he established a photo studio. After a while, when he felt he needed a bigger and better car for his business, he sold the MG and sent me my portion of the sale.

The time came when the house where we rented an apartment was put up for sale, and we found ourselves looking for another place to live. Everywhere we looked, the rent was more than my family was able to pay. We heard there was an area in Winnipeg where new bungalows were being built, and only a small down payment was required. Papa checked it out, saw that we could come up with the down payment, and soon moved us into a new house of our own. With the three of us working, plus Mama taking in sewing, we were able to afford the monthly mortgage payments. We moved in shortly before my twenty-first birthday. During my time at work, Mama embroidered a beautiful landscape picture, which she had framed, and gave it to me for my birthday. Today I have it hanging in our bungalow.

We were so thrilled to finally have our own place to live. The best part for me was that I had my own bedroom, a closet for my few clothes, and privacy. The bathroom had white tiled walls, and everything looked fresh and beautiful. Oh, yes, Papa's two paintings made it into our bungalow, all the way from Russia. The bigger of the two was a scene of nymphs coming out of the water during the night and reaching for the moonlight. The frame of that painting had a bullet hole in it, a souvenir from the war. Mama had originally hung that picture in the living room; however, we noticed that it made visitors uncomfortable because of the nude nymphs. So, Mama replaced it with the smaller painting, which was a pastoral scene of trees and a brook. The bigger picture was hung in the master bedroom.

Mama was able to trade in her old foot-pedal sewing machine for a new portable Elna. She made good use of it by taking in sewing. She was an excellent seamstress, who could duplicate anything from a picture.

Papa built a fence around the bungalow and painted it white. He also landscaped the whole yard himself. He planted trees and perennials in the back yard, and he built a garden bench and placed it behind the house, facing the garden. On both sides of the front door, he planted hybrid climbing tea roses. They covered the better part of the walls. People from the agriculture department at the University of Manitoba stopped by and asked Papa what he did to grow roses that normally would not survive Manitoba's cold climate. His roses also never suffered from black spot. Papa never was selfish with his knowledge of gardening, so he willingly shared the steps he took to successfully grow this particular type of rose. He eventually entered his garden in a competition and won first prize for that year.

Brother Val and I started attending an English Baptist church, where we joined the choir and made friends in the youth group. It was at a young men's baseball game that I met my future husband, Sam Hill. He was athletic, tall, and handsome. He took me home after one of the games. That is when I found out he was pursuing a degree in accounting, and that he also had a part-time job in between his studies. The next time I saw him, he was coming back from a summer camp where he had volunteered as a camp counsellor. After I met his family, I was invited to Sunday dinners quite often. I liked that, because Sam's mother was a very good cook. I can't remember a Sunday when I was there, that there weren't other invited dinner guests as well.

On my birthday the next spring, Sam surprised me with a watch. It was the very first one that I had ever owned. We continued to date, and in June he proposed to me. I accepted. We became engaged and decided to get married the following year, in September. In the meantime, I applied for Canadian citizenship and eventually became a full-fledged Canadian citizen. My parents, after attending English classes in the evenings, became Canadian citizens as well. Now we were no longer "Displaced Persons" or "refugees," but adopted members of Canadian society with all the rights, privileges, and responsibilities of Canadian citizens—yippee!

Our wedding day, September 7, 1956, was fast approaching. Mama made my wedding dress according to a picture I saw in a bridal magazine, with lots of beautiful lace and layers of tulle. She also made my going-away outfit, which was a fitted, cream-coloured dress with a matching coat. With it, I wore a navy-blue, wide-brimmed hat with big pale-pink roses, navy-blue shoes, and a matching purse. Mama also made all the bridesmaids' dresses. Val was the official wedding photographer. My cousin Mary was my maid of honour, and two of my girlfriends were my bridesmaids. Another two girlfriends were candle lighters, and a friend's daughter was the flower girl. Sam's brother Bob was his best man, and two of his best friends were ushers. One of Sam's mother's friends made our wedding cake. Our wedding took place on a beautiful Friday evening, and all went according to plan. Sam's father kindly gave us the family car to use during our honeymoon. We drove as far as Banff, stopping here and there to do some sightseeing. While we were gone, Mama had an open house for the ladies who had attended our wedding, to view all the gifts they had blessed us with. She served them coffee and the butter cream tortes that had been left over from our wedding dinner.

For the first two years of our married life, Sam and I lived with my parents. Our daughter Melody was born during this time. Then we rented four rooms on the second floor of a house that belonged to an elderly lady. She lived on the main floor. During that time, our son Sam Jr. was born. We eventually moved into a small, renovated single house, and while living there, we welcomed our second daughter, Anita, into our lives. After Sam received his CA degree from the University of Manitoba, he worked for the Canada Permanent Trust Company for a while. Eventually, Sam was offered a new job with the Auditor General's department in Ottawa, and we decided it would be a good move for all of us. Our children were five and a half, almost four, and almost two years old. Sam handed in his resignation at the Trust Company, and there was plenty of time before he needed to be in Ottawa to start his new job.

Papa was sixty years old when he bought his first car and learned to drive. He built a garage for his car in one corner of the backyard. Using his artistic touches, he installed two side doors instead of one. His neighbour, who always called him George, asked, "George, why has your garage got two doors?" Papa, with his limited English, had a very simple answer for him: "One is for in and one is for out."

Papa wasn't much for jokes. When he was working up north, he would be gone for two to three weeks at a time. He would read his Bible at night and save his earnings diligently, while the other men gambled some of theirs away playing cards every night. One day, some of the men he was working with played a joke on him. When it was lunchtime, Papa went to grab his lunch pail from where he had placed it that morning and found that it would not move. He opened the lid and discovered the bottom nailed to the table. When he came home and told us about it, we were doubling over with laughter, but he did not think it was funny.

It was during these years in Winnipeg that Mama opened up about her early life in Russia. Before that time, we'd only heard bits and pieces about it once in a while. When we entertained relatives in our backyard on a nice summer day, they would drink coffee and talk about the old days in Russia. Here are some of the stories that I heard Mama tell.

Mama was born in 1907, and when she was six, a terrible epidemic of typhoid fever broke out in Ukraine. It affected Mama's whole village. While her own household was safe from the disease, Grandmama would go from house to house, looking after the sick and dying. Then the disease struck her own family. Mama was the first one to come down with it. As soon as Grandmama noticed the symptoms, she prepared a hot bath for Mama and made her sit on a chair that was put into the tub. Then she was covered with sheets and blankets and put to bed. She woke up two weeks later and found the house to be very still. One of their neighbour ladies was looking after the household because Mama's entire family had come down with the disease. Eventually, every family member became well again.

During the Russian civil war and the 1917 Bolshevik revolution, many of the peasants who had worked for wealthy farmers formed marauding bands that went on a plundering, raping, and killing spree from village to village. They would come riding on horses and would stop at any house and demand that a meal be prepared for them. After eating, they would look around and take anything they liked with them. During these times, Mama's father would go into hiding because they killed many of the village men. On one such occasion, a band of men rode up to Mama's house with the intent to rape the girls. Grandmama did not open the door, so they came to a window where she was standing guard with an axe in her hands. She was not a large woman, but she had a lot of courage. She opened the window and said, "The first man who climbs through the window will have his head chopped off," and she meant it. No doubt God sent angels to protect her family because the aggressors fled.

During the time of the famine in Russia, millions of people starved to death. It was a man-made famine imposed by Stalin. He declared all farm crops and animals state-owned, and drastic measures were meted out to those field workers who dared to take some of the produce home for their families. The village people where Mama lived had their own gardens, but they did not produce enough to feed a large family for a whole year. Also, there was no meat to be found in the stores. Many people in her village died of starvation. Mama tells of the time that Grandmama resorted to butchering their own dog so that the family could have some meat. While cooking the meat, a neighbour lady stopped by to chat with Grandmama. The aroma was wafting through the house, and the lady friend asked what she was cooking. Grandmama did not tell her what it was, but she invited her to stay for dinner because she knew this neighbour was starving. It was after dinner was finished that Grandmama revealed where the meat had come from.

This kind of conversation went on often in our household, but only with people who were born in Russia and who were familiar with the life lived there during those troubled times.

Seven

Ottawa

It was time to start thinking about our move to Ottawa. Sam arranged for the movers to come to our house and pack all our belongings for shipment. After packing the car with the things we would need on our trip, it was time to say our good-byes to the families on both sides. There were a few tears shed, and we left hoping that we had made the right decision for our future.

We arrived in Ottawa in June of 1963, the year that President John F. Kennedy was assassinated. I remember that day well. I happened to be in a grocery store, standing in line to pay the grocery bill, when I first heard the news over the loudspeakers. It was a very emotional day for many people, including myself. I had always felt somehow connected to the United States. After all, had the events after the war turned in our favour, my family would be living somewhere in the U.S. on this very day.

We stayed in a motel during the first few weeks in Ottawa, while we did some house-hunting and sight-seeing. On our first Sunday, we attended a service at the Metropolitan Bible Church downtown, and it became our regular church home. There were programs for the children, and Sam and I joined the choir. We became church members and have helped in many areas of the church ministries throughout the years. Sam enjoyed his job with the Auditor General for fifteen years, after which he and a friend formed a CA partnership, which lasted for twenty-eight years.

As the children got older, I took on a job with a computer firm, where I worked for eleven years. At the suggestion of one of my coworkers, I took up golfing at the age of forty-five. After several weeks of group lessons, Sam and I took out a membership at one of the local golf courses. Golf became the topic of many conversations. I got to love the game and made good use of my membership. It also was a good way to spend time together with Sam. Being a member of a golf club, as well as the Canadian Ladies Golf Association, gave me a chance to play the best courses in the Ottawa area. I became an avid golfer, and I worked hard to break the score of 100. The day I made it happen came eventually, and after my last putt on the eighteenth green, I did a somersault to celebrate my big accomplishment.

Over the next few months, I kept lowering my score and became a Class B golfer. Every summer, there are many golf competitions held in the Ottawa area for female golfers. When I turned fifty years old, I signed up for the Class B Senior tournament. The weather on the day of the competition left much to be desired. It was cloudy, and the forecast was for rain. Sure enough, after playing the first three holes, it began to rain and never stopped; but the competition continued. I was so glad to get into the clubhouse after finishing the eighteenth hole. I handed in my score card, relaxed for a little while, and then headed for home. I did not wait for the last few of the sixty-seven golfers to finish their game. Upon arriving home, I got a call from the club, saying that my score was the lowest and I had won the tournament. Needless to say, I was very pleased—although somewhat surprised—because most of the women I golfed with were seasoned golfers, while I considered myself still fairly new at the game.

While Sam was at work, I would leave early in the morning to start golfing at 7:00 a.m. One day, when I was golfing all by myself and was about to start the second nine holes, I noticed an elderly club member ahead of me, a man I had seen many times before. He was one who usually golfed alone, probably because he had a problem with one of his legs and was not able to walk very quickly. I caught up to him, and he invited me to join him and finish the game together. We ended up having breakfast together.

While conversing, the subject of World War II came up. He asked me where I had been during the war years. After I told him a little bit about myself and mentioned that I had been in Dresden during the time it was bombed, he told me he was on one of the United Kingdom planes that took part in the bombing there, and over the city of Freiburg as well. He told me that now, in his old age, he felt awful about having taken part in the war. He said that, on Remembrance Day, he dons his World War II uniform and speaks at schools about the evils of war.

In my middle age, I was invited to share my life story at a Stonecroft Ministries Christian Women's Club in Ottawa. After my first presentation, I kept getting invitations from other Stonecroft clubs. That kept me busy for the next twenty years. I travelled to most of the towns in Ontario and Northern Ontario, as well as clubs in Quebec, New Brunswick, Nova Scotia, and Prince Edward Island. I was also invited to speak at several clubs in upstate New York. I enjoyed sharing with other women what God has done in my life. I received no pay for doing this, only a small amount of money to cover the cost of gas for my car. Sometimes my husband would come with me, when he wasn't busy at work, and that gave us a chance to spend time together.

I love being outdoors in the summertime. On a nice day, I will spend most of my time working in the garden. I think I inherited the love of gardening from my Papa. One year, a local garden centre in our area invited people to enter their gardens in a competition. There were thirteen gardens that people could visit. Then they cast their votes for the one they liked best. Our garden won first prize by popular vote. I know that if Papa would have seen our garden, he would have been happy to know he had passed the love of gardening to his daughter.

During the years before my husband retired, we took several trips to Europe. There were a few trips to Germany, several to England—where we visited with Sam's sister and family—and one trip to Israel, which we will never forget. It was awesome.

After Sam retired, we started to take short vacations more often. We went on a couple of seven-day cruises and took yearly trips in the fall to the southern United States, where we did some shopping and enjoyed the sunshine.

It was on one of these trips that we decided to take a side trip to Bally, Pennsylvania, the town from which Lizzy Gehman and her two brothers had sent us parcels when my family was in Bamberg after the war. These were also the same people who were ready to sponsor my family to help us get to the United States. At that time, I was thirteen years old. Now, fifty-five years later, would any of the three still be alive? Well, we would soon find out.

We stopped at the Bally post office to ask some questions. There, we were given a list with the phone numbers of seven people named Gehman who lived in Bally. We were also allowed to use one of the post office phones.

I called the first person named Gehman and there was no answer. The same happened with the next five. Then, after I dialed the last number—Bingo! I could tell by the voice that it was an elderly lady who answered my call. After I explained my reason for the call, she said she was not Lizzy Gehman, but she had been married to one of the Gehman brothers, though she was now a widow. As she happened to live just around the corner from the post office, we were invited to come over and see her. She gave us her address, and we got to her house in a couple of minutes. After we told her what this little side trip was all about, she informed us that the rest of that Gehman family, including Lizzy, were no longer around, and if we were interested, the cemetery was close by. She apologized for not being able to treat us to a meal.

We followed her directions to the cemetery and found many gravestones with the Gehman name. Several generations of that family must have lived in Bally. We finally found Lizzy's grave. As my eyes fixed on her gravestone, my thoughts wandered to the times she and her brothers had blessed my family with so many good things, packed lovingly into the parcels we received from them during those hard times after the war. In my mind, I said, Thank you, and hoped that God would reward them for their kindness.

My parents visited Ottawa several times, coming all the way from British Columbia, where they had moved a few years after we left Winnipeg. They loved it there. Papa could grow all kinds of plants that would not grow in Winnipeg due to the cold Manitoba winters. They found a church they liked, and there they met many people they had known in Russia. Both parents joined a seniors' choir because they loved to sing. Papa got a job in Seattle, where he worked on industrial buildings as a steamfitter and plumber. He would leave for work on a Sunday afternoon and return on Friday afternoon. He always left a love note for Mama, and occasionally upon returning, he would surprise her with a present. After he retired, you would find him working in his garden. In the evenings, he put on his earphones and listened to his classical music.

When I think of Papa, I realize that he actually had several hobbies. Besides gardening and classical music, he also liked to read. While belonging to a book-of-the-month club, he acquired many books to his liking. He and Mama both loved art, and they purchased several paintings during their years of retirement.

I think my brothers and I inherited some of our parents' talents. My brother Val became a photographer and owned a portrait studio in Vancouver. He also liked to garden and loved to sing. I inherited my love of gardening from Papa and my love of sewing and singing from Mama. However, it was my brother Alex who inherited all the talents of both my parents.

Alex loved music, and he also had a good voice. When he was only three yeas old, he would stop whatever he was doing and listen to the music that came from the record player. In his adult years, he could play many musical instruments without ever having had a lesson. He was good with his hands: for a certain antique lover, he made beautiful furniture that looked antique. He also did some paintings, of which I own two.

When I think of my parents, I am glad they enjoyed some good years in Canada. Papa passed away a few days after his eightieth birthday. After selling their house, Mama moved into a condo, where she lived for two years before moving into a nursing home for the last years of her life.

Both my brothers married in Canada and had families. Alex suffered a stroke in his senior years and passed away a year later. Val also had health issues in his later years, and he passed away from heart failure.

One last note about Papa's two paintings that followed us all the way from Russia to Canada: The canvas of the large painting of the nymphs was removed from the frame with the bullet hole in it and sold. It was replaced with a needlepoint that Mama embroidered during her retirement years. It eventually found a place in Val's house. The smaller painting of a landscape was given to Alex.

I am thankful I was adopted by this country. I have a Canadian passport that does not look any different from my neighbour's Canadian passport. No persons in Canada are labelled subhuman by the government because of their race or religion.

I am thankful to God, who protected me from harm during the war years and is allowing me now to live in peace. War is always about loss of life. Jesus came to this earth to give life. He died on the cross for the whole world, thereby assuring everyone who believes in him of eternal life.

I came to this country with no money, no degrees, no diplomas, very little formal education, and poverty of faith. I can truly say that God has replenished what the ravages of the war years took away from me.

To God be the glory!

Epilogue

A few years ago, my husband and I downsized to a two-bedroom bungalow. We have a small yard that we can take care of ourselves, and where I can putter around with plants. On a hot summer day, we can enjoy our lunch on the front porch of the house where it's cool and shady. Our house backs onto a conservation area, where there are many birds that we can watch and listen to as we sit on our back deck.

We still attend our church, travel a little, read books, and watch TV programs to our liking. Whenever we can, we spend time with our family. Our children are married to great spouses, and all of them, like us, are retired. We have three grown grandchildren who are the pride and joy of our lives.

www.ingramcontent.com/pod-product-compliance
Lightning Source LLC
Chambersburg PA
CBHW072024040426
42447CB00009B/1719